KU-686-795

Flight of the Phoenix

Soaring to Success in the 21st Century

12686274
CHESTER COLLEGE
ACC. No. 0105740
DEPT.
LIBRARY
WITHDRAWN

John Whiteside
and
Sandra Egli

Butterworth—Heinemann
Boston   Oxford   Johannesburg   Melbourne   New Delhi   Singapore

Copyright © 1997 by John A. Whiteside and Sandra R. Egli.

A member of the Reed Elsevier group.

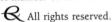 All rights reserved.

No part of this publication may be reproduced, stored in a retrieval system, or transmitted in any form or by any means, electronic, mechanical, photocopying, recording, or otherwise, without the prior written permission of the publisher.

Recognizing the importance of preserving what has been written, Butterworth–Heinemann prints its books on acid-free paper whenever possible.

Library of Congress Cataloging-in-Publication Data
Whiteside, John, 1946–
    Flight of the Phoenix: soaring to success in the 21st century /
John Whiteside and Sandra Egli.
        p. cm
    Includes bibliographical references and index.
    ISBN 0-7506-9798-9 (pbk.)
        1. Management.   2. Success in business.   3. Management—Case studies.   4. Problem
solving—Case studies.   I. Egli, Sandra, 1947– .   II. Title.
HD31.W5124   1996
650.1—dc20   96-20995
                                                                                                CIP

British Library Cataloguing-in-Publication Data
A catalogue record for this book is available from the British Library.

The publisher offers special discounts on bulk orders of this book.
For information, please contact:
Manager of Special Sales
Butterworth–Heinemann
313 Washington Street
Newton, MA 02158–1626
Tel: 617-928-2500
Fax: 617-928-2620

For information on all Business publications available, contact our World Wide Web home
page at: http://www.bh.com/bb

10 9 8 7 6 5 4 3 2 1

Printed in the United States of America

Also by John Whiteside

THE PHOENIX AGENDA: POWER TO TRANSFORM YOUR WORKPLACE

John Wiley & Sons, 1993

FLIGHT OF THE PHOENIX is dedicated to working people who believe in their hearts that there is a way for us to work together in peace and harmony, and who have the commitment and courage to search until they find the way. Especially, we mention these few:

Kevin Wilt   Gracie Williams   Pete Scharfenberg

Ken Knipe   Ray Harness   Michael Duhart

Mike Benhase   Dave Barger

CONTENTS

Acknowledgements

We are grateful that our world is filled with kindred spirits. They are the many people who identify with the message of this book. Some of them have shared their stories and experience in these pages. They have reviewed and made suggestions to improve and clarify the message. They have stood by each of us personally, providing support and courage. They are the people who have taught and helped us to grow. We thank each of you from the bottom of our hearts.

Any book recounting the stories of 21st-century people must begin with an acknowledgement of three exemplary 21st-century men of our acquaintance: *Ray Harness, Ken Knipe,* and *Kevin Wilt.* Without their trust in the efficacy of this message and their courage to take the chance, most of the events in this book would never have taken place.

We also thank *Mike Benhase, Michael Duhart, Pete Scharfenberg* and *Gracie Williams.* They have contributed to this book with stories and reviews. They have also taken the ideas presented here and squeezed them out, shook them up and made them their own. You have our admiration, fellowship, and friendship for life.

We acknowledge two masters of 21st-century communication who contributed to this book: *Peter Conklin,* who died in April 1995, and *Wayne Martsen,* who is alive and kicking. Peter made a great contribution to the revival of Digital Equipment Corporation through the Alpha-chip. Wayne is an unshakeable commitment to bring out the best in everyone.

Our thanks goes to all of the wonderful people in Toledo whose stories grace the pages of this book: *Dave Barger, Skip Blachowski, Wayne Clive, Sharon Detaeye, Chrystal Ellis, Bill Epperson, Brenda Facey, Gordon Gilmer, Joe Goodell, Ken Griffin, Rosalyn Heath, Curt Howard, Patricia Kennedy, Dal Lawrence, Fran Lawrence, Stephanie Lucio, Gary McBride, Dave McClellan, Randy McElfresh, Bud Morgan, Jimmy Neu, Dave Sanderson, Pete Scharfenberg, Darren Smith,* and *Jacqueline Williams.*

Our appreciation also to our dear friends and family who carefully reviewed the drafts of this book as well as contributed their own experiences to be added to its pages. They have been like midwives, bringing this creation into the world: *Alexandra Corson, Peter Evans, Janet Faith, Roger Faith, Tom Kolepp, Wayne Pennycook, Louis Rekers, Lana Ruch, John Russett, Pat Sheean, Marcus Wilson,* and *Karen Yamada.*

A special thanks to *Steve Egli* and *Holly Whiteside,* who read many versions and drafts and more important, stood by us through the frustrations and challenges of this undertaking.

And from Sandra: *To John Whiteside,* the best ever business partner who daily reminds me of my greatness; *To my parents, Louis and Virginia Rekers,* I can never thank you enough or adequately express my appreciation and love for all you have given to me. *And to Eileen Bowden,* my deepest love and gratitude for helping me express more of who I truly am.

Preface

FLIGHT OF THE PHOENIX: SOARING TO SUCCESS IN THE 21ST CENTURY shows how to master and thrive on destabilizing changes sweeping across the workplace. This book gives tools and a new way of solving problems, especially for individuals and companies in search of a better way to work. It shows how to heal the wounds of reengineering and downsizing and presents a positive vision for the 21st-century workplace.

This is a time of great opportunity. As a society, we have moved beyond the struggle for food. We have created material wealth for ourselves. What is possible now? Could employees and managers, working together, find a way to bring greater satisfaction to work and reclaim meaningful personal lives, and in doing so actually increase the value of their contributions?

This book shows a new perspective that puts corporate and individual needs in synergy, rather than in opposition. The only tools we need to apply this perspective are speaking and listening, for language creates reality.

The idea that language creates reality was introduced by John Whiteside in his book, THE PHOENIX AGENDA: POWER TO TRANSFORM YOUR WORKPLACE. In that book, John outlined twelve communication tools for creating *a great day at work, one day at a time* for you and the people around you. You do not need to read the earlier book to gain the full benefit of this book. However, if you are familiar with *The Phoenix Agenda*, you will recognize the foundation it provides here. The thesis of THE PHOENIX AGENDA is that language does not describe an independent reality; language creates reality.

Each of the 12 themes of THE PHOENIX AGENDA is a way to create new realities through generous listening and committed speaking:
- *Generate Trust: Use this conversation to offer trust freely as a gift, not as a reward for the past.*
- *Uncover Context: Use this conversation to surface underlying and unspoken assumptions.*

- *Invent the Future: Use this conversation to engage and inspire people with a vision of the future.*
- *Articulate Strategies: Use this practical conversation to overcome obstacles and discover step-by-step approaches to fulfill a vision.*
- *Source Action: Use this conversation to initiate action that consistently leads to accomplishment and results.*
- *Exploit Moments of Truth: In every setback there is an opportunity to accelerate the achievement of goals. Use this conversation to take advantage of setbacks.*
- *Maintain Awareness: Use this conversation to place goals and plans on public display, to assure they are remembered, followed, and accomplished.*
- *Realize Results: Use this conversation to recognize the outcomes of projects and plans, both successes and failures, to pave the way for new goals.*
- *Create Wisdom: Use this conversation to crystallize learning, and to share it for the benefit of all.*
- *Transcend Addictions: Use this conversation to let go of automatic and unproductive behaviors and allow them to be replaced with effective alternatives.*
- *Complete the Past: Use this conversation to acknowledge the accomplishments and failures of the past in order to let them go.*
- *Acknowledge Freely: Use this conversation to express appreciation and honor for people.*

FLIGHT OF THE PHOENIX: SOARING TO SUCCESS IN THE 21ST CENTURY presents and demonstrates the power of communication to create the work world you desire. Part I of the book, *Challenging the Culture of Work*, is an inquiry into what you take for granted about the workplace and your relationship to work today. This section raises questions and opens up a valuable examination for every reader.

Chapter 1, *Your Colleagues in Crisis*, tells the stories of successful people whose work lives are in transition. Their experiences illuminate what is happening in the workplace today in a way that statistics cannot.

Chapter 2, *Why Work?* examines the relationship between employers and employees. What holds them together, and where do profits come from?

Chapter 3, *Could Work Be Wonderful?* tells the stories of companies and individuals who have discovered new and rewarding ways to work together.

Part II, *A Better Way To Work*, presents the perspectives and tools to make your world of work both exciting and hopeful. You will benefit greatly by taking the time to answer the questions posed for you as you read this section.

Chapter 4, *The Power of Perspectives*, shows the havoc played in human affairs as a consequence of judging human behavior according to limited individual perspectives of right and wrong.

Chapter 5, *Fulfill Your Future*, presents key aspects of 21st-century perspective and illustrates how 21st-century thinking can help you build strong, positive, and productive relationships.

Chapter 6, *The Only Two Tools You Will Ever Need*, looks at the power of speaking and listening to create reality. It extends the themes of THE PHOENIX AGENDA to include new ways to listen and thus increase your appreciation for other perspectives.

Part III, *Tools for 21st-Century Work*, shows how to use 21st-century thinking to make powerful friends, create wealth, and heal disputes.

Chapter 7, *Create Powerful Connections*, outlines nine specific and common perspectives found in business. It shows how to appreciate other perspectives and develop genuine relationships with people whose perspectives are different from your own.

Chapter 8, *Create Real Results*, shows how to achieve what you want. It examines the myth of measurement and presents a variation on themes from THE PHOENIX AGENDA designed to focus on producing meaningful results.

Chapter 9, *Dissolve Any Dispute*, addresses the fundamental question of what goes wrong in human relationships and how to set relationships right.

Our purpose in writing FLIGHT OF THE PHOENIX is to provide you an opportunity to rethink and redesign your worklife for the 21st century. Does your work call forth from you all that you have to offer in the brief span of years you are alive? For most people, the work world takes advantage of only a fraction of their full range of talents. We hope that what you take away from reading this book is a beginning and an opportunity to use your real talents fully.

We intend this book to be practical and positive; by detailing the day-to-day actions of ordinary workers at all levels, we show how these actions can be realistically altered and improved to create a better workplace.

About the Stories

All the stories in this book are factual. The majority are from our own experience or the experiences of our colleagues as told to us. The few stories drawn from public sources are so indicated. Some of the stories use real names and locations; others are altered for the privacy of the participants. Only where we have used a full name, first and last, is it the actual name of the person. All other names are fictionalized. Sometimes the location has been changed, but all of the workplaces exist. Everyone mentioned in the book wants their story, their experience, to contribute to your success.

How to Get the Most from This Book

Many friends and colleagues have read this book for us before publication. All of them have said, *This is not a book to skim or race through.* About half the early reviewers chose to read the book a second or third time and observed that their reactions and thinking evolved with each reading. The power of the book lies in your thoughtfulness and assimilation of the message. This power will become available to you when you take the time to think penetratingly about *your* work, *your* future, *your* goals. What is it that you want to happen for you at work and in your life? Whether you have the desire to make a major mark in your profession or simply wish to live in harmony with people, you will get more out of the book by participating in the inquiries and by answering the questions based upon the issues you face in your life today. This book is written to make a difference for you on an everyday basis.

One reviewer read the ball-toss exercise (Chapter 4, Try a New Perspective) at the same time he was teaching his six-year-old son the rudiments of hitting a softball. He used the exercise with his son and was filled with fatherly pride when the exercise was a complete success. In his words, *Carl didn't just hit the ball, he crushed it!*

Please read this book in the order that suits you. There is no absolute reason to move from front to back. Part I makes sense of the background of current business conditions and trends as we interpret them. Part II provides the foundation and in-depth tools for 21st-century success. Part III is for those action-oriented readers who want to jump into the case studies and observe 21st-century thinking in action. There is no one right place to begin and each part of the message leads to the others.

We are glad you are here. Welcome. It has been a privilege and an honor to write this book for you.

Part I

Challenging the Culture of Work

He that loveth silver shall not be satisfied with silver; nor he that loveth abundance with increase; this is also vanity.

. . . ECCLESIASTES

I

Your Colleagues in Crisis

> Seneca thinks the gods are well pleased when they see great men
> contending with adversity.
>
> ... ROBERT BURTON, *The Anatomy of Melancholy, 1651*

WHAT WILL BECOME OF US?

What will become of us? How will it turn out with our careers, our
companies, our mortgages, our families, and our lives?

As the second Industrial Revolution sweeps across the world and
threatens to reengineer everyone out of a job, what is to become of us
and what are we to do now that the rules of the game of life, work, survival, and success have changed?

The popular press, as a whole, paints a dismal picture of the future:
a declining middle class with stagnant wages and increasing, permanent
layoffs; uncertainty and angst among the middle managerial class; and
the basic value of loyalty to the organization gone. We seem to have re-
defined the purpose of business as the increase of short-term shareholder value, at the expense of employee, customer, and community.

Life seemed pretty stable 20 years ago. That was a time when people worked for the system. We automatically agreed with the boss,

believed in the company, and looked forward to a lifetime of steady paychecks and suburban living. Since those quiet times, we have been riding waves of international competition, quality movements, re-engineering, restructuring, downsizing, and rightsizing, in cycles of ever-increasing intensity.

But wait! What if you could work, not at the mercy of the latest consultants' fad or top-management fashion, but for meaningful and deeply held principles, and reasons that you invent for yourself? Maybe you are not just at the mercy of trends. Maybe you have some say in the outcome, for your career, for your company, and even for the future of the working life in general. Someone has to invent trends. Why not you?

What if work could be productive and profitable both for the shareholders *and* for you?

This book is designed for readers who want to be proactive, not reactive, in shaping the 21st century for themselves and their companies. We start this exercise in soaring, not with statistics, but with stories of real people who are finding their way into the 21st century. As you will see, every person's story contains success. And in every case, the rules of the game have changed and the person faces uncertainty. But beyond the uncertainty, are the seeds of new beginnings.

The book shows how to nurture these beginnings, to have them grow into major opportunities for yourself and your company. But for the moment, listen to the stories. You may be interested to see how other career-oriented men and women are coping with corporate reengineering, business reinvention, and vanishing lifetime careers. Perhaps, in places, you will see yourself.

CAREERS AT THE CROSSROADS

Fresh out of school in the late 1960s, Ed's first job is selling hot new minicomputers. He is excited to work for one of the first companies to offer an alternative to IBM's mainframes. He is so proud when he participates in his first deal. Ed is always excited about his latest project, and he earns his promotion to management. It is a great challenge, but he learns and masters that job, too. In the process he acquires the accouterments of upper-middle-class life. You may think he has it made.

Many years pass. Then one day there is an unexpected twist. Ed is no longer so enthusiastic. He seems to lose his clarity and focus. Watching his son surf the Internet, Ed feels a little over his head and wonders whether the world of technology has passed him by. Then he loses his job. It may be a while before he finds another and he learns to browse the Internet for himself as part of his search for work.

Can you relate to Karen? She is a remarkable woman, a top-notch professional, and the highest-ranking engineer in the division. Her ideas and opinions are respected throughout the company. Her decisions affect products for tens of thousands of customers. She is a role model and her advice is always sought.

Then events conspire. Her company is under fire and goes through a terrible time. Markets the company has controlled for years are lost overnight. Half of the company disappears; Karen's colleagues leave or are laid off. Her job is safe but something fundamental has shifted. Karen has always valued most her community of friends and colleagues on the job. With so many of them laid off, the loyalty, the spark, and excitement are gone for her. It takes a while but one day she speaks for the first time of launching herself on an entirely new career.

Then there is Roger. He works for 18 years at a flour mill. Straight from high school, he starts as a sweeper and eventually learns the maintenance requirements of the entire plant. At every opportunity he learns new skills and acquires new levels of certification. He is a union representative for the plant, too. Then, with no warning at all, the mill closes. Roger suffers most for the people around him. They cannot understand the shutdown. Officially, of course, the reason is cost cutting. Roger has a wife and two sons and, for them, he accepts the job offered by the company in another city. But he leaves behind his parents, sisters, aunts, uncles, and a network of family and history that can never be replaced.

Pat spends years coming up through the ranks, beginning on the plant floor during his college vacations. No one works harder than he does, and he rises to head the operations of the entire company. Pat not only survives downturns—he saves the company, several times reinventing the business. When the calculator market turns unprofitable, for example, he switches his plant to manufacturing night-vision equipment for the military. Later, he anticipates the decrease in military spending and launches a line of 3-dimensional X-ray imaging devices for dentists. His crowning achievement, of which he is most proud, is forging a cooperative working relationship with the union. Today, it bothers him that no one seems to remember these past achievements. Now, the company is searching for a new president and it looks as though he will be passed over. Could this temporary setback mean he will fulfill a lifetime dream to build his own company? He is beginning to speak about that now.

Is change a powerful source of opportunity?

Have you known someone like Gracie? She comes, in 1965, from the South with her husband pursuing the promise of jobs to support themselves and their children. In the 1960s, a lot of companies will not even hire a woman until she is 21. She has to wait for her birthday to start work. But, the years are good for them, and today both their daughters are in college. Gracie is a union representative, and with automation facing the plant she sees a difficult and painful time ahead for many people. It occurs to her that she can help people make the transition. Perhaps no one has to be lost in the shuffle. She applies for a job as a trainer for the complex new equipment and is accepted.

Have you known someone as remarkable as Otis? He comes from a family of Texas sharecroppers. Now he runs the international sales organization for a major high-tech firm and has amassed a net worth of five million dollars. He is a great salesman and one of the most successful managers of engineering and manufacturing. He puts his heart and soul into his job, and truly sacrifices everything for the company. In a company with the usual competitive and political struggles, he is known for sharing authority and power, for calling on people to give their best effort every day. The loyalty he inspires is a testament to his commitment to people. But Otis is tired of pursuing success just to prove something. His children will soon be grown, and he wants to stop spending 30 weeks a year traveling around the world. He is thinking about what might be next for him and whether he has the courage to walk away from this position he gave so much to attain.

WHAT IS GOING ON HERE?

Take stock. Look in the mirror. Consider your colleagues. You have worked hard and so have they. We have all faced challenges, battles, and milestones and we have done well. Still, some say there is rough water ahead. A major upheaval is in progress in society and the workplace. The analysts' assessments of this upheaval are alarmist and depressing. Experts say that workplace loyalty is dead, that tension and anxiety will become the norm for everyone who depends on work for a living. Corporate managers are strategizing about self-survival in the new and future corporation.

> Survival is a game that everyone loses.

This public conversation has an everyone-for-themselves quality. According to current wisdom, secure jobs and lifelong employment are dead so everyone must plot their own course, brace for hard times, and act like an independent business. Such advice leaves us isolated and alienated from one another and in a state of predatory watchfulness. But, we are more connected to one another than such an outlook admits. As one survivor of corporate layoffs put it, *I did not like some of the people who were laid off. Still, it hurt to see them go. These were my workmates, some for many years. I cannot feel good except that each of them does well in the future.*

What is going on? Is the work world as we have known it gone forever? What do we face in the future? Certainly, the 20th-century working arrangements that gave a measure of stability and order are falling away. Hierarchy, definite lifelong career paths, and organizational structures dissolve beneath our feet. Often, it seems, they are replaced simply by a different hierarchy with now murky lines of advancement. We wonder how we can feel good about our jobs again. Is it wise to be loyal and dedicated to the company? What does the company owe us, or anyone? What skills make us desirable to other companies? Is there a way out of the rat race, or must we run twice as fast just to keep our jobs? And for those of us left in traditional jobs, how do we effectively manage people who face these dilemmas?

Sometimes, questions have easy answers. But these questions arise because of a fundamental shift in the social order, in how we expected life to turn out. We can answer such questions only if we look into the background of assumptions, culture, and expectations from which the questions arise in the first place.

Asking a question in a new way is worth a dozen answers.

This book introduces the art of asking questions in a deep, productive way. We will raise questions such as: *What is the purpose of a company? Why do you work? What is the meaning of measurement? Are you certain that A causes B?* Within the new domains, you will find yourself inventing exciting and valuable questions for your worklife.

Consider these stories of workers embracing the 21st century. Ken, a manufacturing vice president in a high-tech firm has no manufacturing facilities to oversee. After years in a large corporation, he is delighted that he is now free to make deals with independent suppliers. As he tells it: *In the old corporation, I had 200 people reporting to me but also layers of bureaucratic limitations placed upon what I could actually do. Now I have 10 people reporting to me but I wheel and deal with 20 suppliers who collectively represent several thousand workers!*

How did Ken make this change? He rephrased the question, *How can I get another job as a manufacturing vice president?*, into a new and searching inquiry: *How can I use my expertise in a way that is exciting and fun for me?*

We introduced Pat a few pages ago. He was wondering whether to leave his company if he was passed over for the position of president. Fortunately, Pat asked himself a deeper question, *What do I want to do in my career that I haven't yet done?* Asking the question this way gave him the courage to leave his job to fulfill the dream of owning his own business. Pat is today the president of a newly founded firm manufacturing artificial limbs and joints. What does this opportunity to play in a free market look like for him? His first and most critical role is salesman for the company's products. While he is engaged in selling, his two co-founders are, with their own hands, machining the limbs and filling orders. He is happier than he has been in years.

James has chosen to stay with his corporation. But he recently took stock of his take-no-prisoners management style that got him where he is today and is asking himself, *Is this really the way I want to manage? Is this the best thing for me, my company, and our customers?* Thinking about it in this way, he has decided to shift directions, to master the skills of mentoring, listening, and building a dynamic workforce by gentle yet powerful listening. The productivity in his office is improving in ways he never expected or imagined.

COULD CHANGE RENEW US?

Feelings of fear, self-doubt, anxiety, and anger are exactly the same emotions experienced by people living in the Soviet Union at the time the communist government collapsed. Prior to the fall, people had the security of knowing the rules for surviving within the system. But the security came with a price: a lack of opportunity in business and personal expression, limitations on income, and the unavailability of many goods and services. After the fall, opportunities for business creativity and entrepreneurism skyrocketed. The cap on future income and the availability of goods lifted. But, freedom, too, has a price. The price is not knowing the rules or even where next month's rent will come from. What will it be—freedom or security?

The opposite of security is freedom.

Dramatic changes may be frightening but also exciting; they demand that we demonstrate our finest skills. Ethnographers have determined that at one time some North American Indian tribes moved every 25 to 30 years. The tribal leaders ordered the move when life became too easy and predictable. People were apathetic. They needed the challenge of building new homes and finding new sources of food and clothing. The change brought renewed purpose and meaning and demanded that people reach beyond their old ways to create new ways. Considering that people in the United States move on average every four years, are we so different?

What if the most significant outcome of our current economic turmoil and trauma is renewed purpose and power in our lives? Is it possible that we are being reawakened to our connections and caring for one another? Is it possible that this crisis is exactly what we need in our lives?

20TH- VERSUS 21ST-CENTURY THINKING

To the darkness defined and described by the economic analysts and news media, we say *Phooey!* and instead issue a challenge and offer an alternative. The alternative is to be accountable for yourself, your circumstances, your life, your results, what goes on around you, and ultimately, the world. This may seem an impossible order. In the latter decades of the 20th century we have stopped taking responsibility even for ourselves, choosing instead to blame our parents, the authorities, people who are not fair to us, and all sorts of circumstances beyond our control. But if the world is to change, only we ourselves can do it. Who else could it be? And that is the subject of this book.

> **If you choose to be accountable for your world without regard for the circumstances you face, this book tells you how to set about creating the events and circumstances you want in your life.**

This book draws a distinction between 20th-century and 21st-century thinking. Twentieth-century thinking is thinking that has us wash our hands, pass the buck, say *not me*, and see ourselves as victims.

> **Twenty-first-century thinking is thinking that creates the world.**

At the heart of 21st-century thinking is the choice to be accountable for creating the world. It is *the-buck-stops-here, that-is-my-job,* and *I-can-do-it* thinking. The people we have drawn on for our examples have made this choice to take charge of their own circumstances.

If you have made a similar choice, this book gives you tools and insights to help and support you. If you have not yet chosen autonomy, this book is an invitation to create the rest of your life and the world in which you choose to live.

How can you direct your own destiny? The process begins with recognizing the power of your own speaking, with knowing you create your life by the power of what you say. If you choose to be accountable, say aloud:

> **I am my word. My word is my bond.**

That is all there is to it. You have taken the oath of accountability. Listen to yourself now as powerful and creative. And above all else, say nothing, absolutely nothing that you do not wish to be true. You might think of it as though you have a genie who, starting now, follows you and grants everything you say; it will all come true.

Do not shrink from or fear this power. It is rightfully yours and this book is about how to use it.

Now, in possession of your new-found power, what do you intend to create? Write down what you would like to have in your professional or personal life that you do not yet have. You can revise and add to what you have written as you read this book, and getting started now is valuable. Consider these innovative business leaders as examples worth emulating.

Mark runs a plant that produces a significant percentage of the world's supply of cereal. A manager of extensive experience, he knows how to compute cost per case, how to work with unions, when to replace his machinery, and how to control the bottom line. Yet what really drives him, what he sees is possible, is this: *I want to run a plant where everyone comes to work every day glad to be there.*

Charlene boasts impeccable credentials in high-technology management. She is currently CEO of a Silicon Valley startup, that makes computer switching equipment. She has seen the market value of her company grow from nothing to $250 million in the year she has worked there. What is her vision? *I'm proudest of the work culture we have created. People are open and friendly and feel a sense of community with each other. That is what I am building and what I want to remain after I move on to other things.*

Roy, operations vice president of a successful high-pressure seal and valve manufacturer and distributor puts it another way: *Motivated people beat capital any day.*

These successful workers and executives are exploring new possibilities for the 21st-century workplace. Throughout FLIGHT OF THE PHOENIX, we explore the new ways of doing business that these pioneers and their colleagues are creating. We show that what others call a workplace crisis is actually a golden opportunity for employers and workers radically to rethink their strategies and their community contract with themselves and each other. The stakes are high and the possible rewards great. Workers and employers have the opportunity to design a new work contract, to design working lives based as much on fulfillment and connection as on earning a living. Corporations have the opportunity to rethink their basic missions. Upper management has the chance to explore and embrace true visionary leadership. Unions have an opportunity to become a community for the future.

But to see these opportunities may require basic recalibration of perspectives. The next chapter explores the question—*why work?*—as it relates to both companies and individuals. We examine why people work and why companies are in business. We will look at whether the bottom line is a metric sophisticated enough for corporate success and whether a steady paycheck is sufficient exchange for our hearts and minds, in the 21st century.

2

Why Work?

Work is love made visible. And if you cannot work with love but only with distaste, it is better that you should leave your work and sit at the gate of the temple and take alms of those who work with joy.

... KAHIL GIBRAN, *The Prophet*

WHAT HOLDS THE WORKPLACE TOGETHER?

Why do you work? Or conversely, why are you in business? Some people are attracted by challenge, some by excitement, some by money, some by intriguing problems, some by a desire to contribute, some by a chance to bring people together, some by the lure of power, and others by the prospect of dramatic adventure. It spells trouble if citizens of a workplace do not share, or at least appreciate, each other's motivations. For example, at the start of a strategic software project, the new vice president, from sales, comes to speak to the seasoned engineers he now leads. *Let's all work hard and make the stock price go up*, he says. But his enticement falls on deaf ears. These are senior engineers, the elite of their profession. They can have any job they want. The professional thrill for

14

them is facing and overcoming sophisticated technical challenges. Instead of addressing this, the vice president turns his people off with what they consider to be crass motivations.

If you are like most people, you work for a number of reasons, some generous, some self-centered, but all profound. Or is it just for a paycheck? Consider the retired research chemist, the father of eight children, who says to his daughter, *You might think that I worked so hard all those years because I had to support the family. Actually, I worked so hard because I loved my job.*

Similarly, if you own a business, or manage in one, why do you do what you do? Is it for profit exclusively? Or are you like the Chicago plant manager who, even though he is hard as nails on budgets and cost control, also says: *Leadership is something bigger than having a job or producing a business result. For me, it is a calling.*

These questions would be valuable at any time, but right now, they are crucial. That is because the workplace is undergoing the most profound change since the Industrial Revolution.

WHY DO COMPANIES HAVE EMPLOYEES?

Today, it is not always clear why companies have employees. It used to be clear. It used to be common for corporate leaders to say that *we are in business to maximize shareholder return, certainly, but we are also in business to make sure that employees and communities do well.* In other words, besides a wage or salary, companies took upon themselves to provide other benefits including, importantly, job security. But public figures from both sides of the political spectrum say today that job security and reciprocal loyalty *are dead.* The workplace ethic that has fueled economic expansion and rising lifestyles for most of the 20th century has disappeared.

Loyalty served the business world, employers and employees alike, for many decades. It is 1978 and an upper-level manager from American Telephone and Telegraph (AT&T) is teaching a class of bright computer science students. He shows slides about the PHONE COMPANY (in 1978 AT&T is the phone company) showing inspired workers nurturing and building the entire nation's communications capability. He ends his speech literally in tears with the words, *I love the* PHONE COMPANY.

Fast forward to today. AT&T is in the middle of the most publicized layoff in history. The company is family no more.

What do corporate leaders say today about their employees? FORTUNE MAGAZINE looked at the 50 companies that had the largest layoffs during 1995.[1] Taken together, these 50 companies laid off a total of about 375,000 employees. FORTUNE then reviewed the annual reports for these companies to learn what their chairmen say about the employees. According to their signed letters, the CEOs value their employees highly, considering them as the company's most important asset and giving them credit for skill, dedication and hard work.

So companies say they value employees at the same time they are getting rid of many of them. Which reveals the true values and goals of corporate leadership: the annual reports or the layoff statistics?

Public figures as diverse as Robert Reich and Patrick Buchanan unite in a harsh conclusion. They say that today the company is the agent of the shareholder alone and will undertake any action that will result in higher stock prices, even if only in the short term. Companies used to downsize when they were in trouble and had no alternative. Today, downsizing is common even in profitable companies.

This trend has generated heavy anti-business press coverage. A NEWSWEEK cover reads CORPORATE KILLERS and the article features unflattering pictures of corporate executives who between them have laid off close to a million employees and who, according to the story, are proud of that achievement.[2]

> If a company does not value its employees above profit, do you suppose it values customers or product quality above profit?

---

[1] "Watch What We Did, Not What We Said," by Thomas A. Stewart, *Fortune Magazine*, April 15, 1996, 140-141.
[2] "The Hit Men," by Alan Sloan, *Newsweek*, Feb. 26, 1996, 44ff.

Whether corporate greed and employee alienation are realities or myths is open to interpretation and debate. Practically, it may not matter. Perception is reality and many companies, as they reengineer, have either fundamentally shifted their basic values or have done a poor job of communicating the values they do hold and the reasons for their actions. Similarly, employees are confused about why they work. As one recently laid-off employee of a high-tech giant says, *I had lived and breathed this company, gave it everything. I was so proud to wear the badge. Now I have dreams about blowing the place up with dynamite.*

Are we moving to an era where companies and employees no longer have common goals?

WHY DO PEOPLE WORK FOR COMPANIES?

Why do people want to work for someone else? At one time it was clear, perhaps it is no longer. The first page of the IBM employment agreement from the 1960s contains a promise of lifetime employment. Yet by as early as the mid-1980s, the employee manual at Apple Computer says that, employees should have no expectation of long-term employment. So the enticements of working for a mega-corporation are not so obvious today.

Consider the case of a middle-aged programmer who maintains old programs written in obsolete computer languages. As long as there are customers who use these outdated systems, this man is valuable, even essential, to his employer. Once the systems are shut down for the last time, this programmer has no value to his company nor, possibly, to many other companies. His manager may appreciate his dedication, but the manager may be gone himself, before the programmer has outlived his usefulness. As painful as it is to consider, the day will come when it will make financial sense to let him go and hire someone fresh from school. It is not that the company is doing anything wrong or immoral.

The company is following common and accepted practices of business today.

From the programmer's perspective, would he be better off as a contractor, making big bucks today and socking it away for tomorrow? Working as a contractor, aware of the need to prepare for the future, is he more likely to remain in tune with the market and to continually update his skills?

Marie has been bravely exploring the new work world. She is a systems analyst who loves her work. Her excellence as an analyst earns her a promotion to management. The job starts out well, but becomes a nightmare of budgets and project-cost accounting. For years she feels trapped and eventually decides to change careers and become a financial advisor. Her goal is to help prepare people for early retirement and enable them to get out of the daily grind that she has come to hate. A year later, although she is an excellent financial advisor, she admits she is not cut out to make cold calls and to sell herself. She decides to return to the computer field. But during her sojourn, she came to enjoy the independence of self-employment. So, she goes into business for herself and returns to her prior employer as a contractor. Once again, she is doing the analytical work that she loves. She makes a lot of money, even more than she did as a manager. And, as she knows, *This gives me the best of both worlds. I get to do what I enjoy and I'm not trapped in the bureaucracy*. Marie did not just get out of management, she put herself in charge of her career. As a middle manager her future was uncertain. As a systems analyst with project management experience, she is *hot property*. Marie is navigating a changing work world, discovering how to work for herself. The company, for its part, is engaged in the same process, trying to figure out when to hire employees and when to outsource.

Each of us can benefit by examining our careers and future thoughtfully, as the programmer needs to do and as Marie did. There are not fewer jobs available, only fewer *steady* jobs. It is up to us to bridge the gaps and create our own sustenance-and-wealth-producing opportunities for the 21st century.

THE FALLACY OF THE BOTTOM LINE

Measurement Is Mischievous

In 1752, England switched from the Julian to the modern Gregorian calendar. The older Julian calendar, in use for hundreds of years up to that point, does not precisely match the solar year, with the consequence that the natural seasons got more and more out of synchrony with the dates on the calendar. So in 1752 England eliminated 11 days. The date jumped 11 days overnight (similar to what happens when we move our clocks ahead an hour for daylight savings time). Distraught peasants, convinced that time itself had been stolen from them, cried in the streets.

Today we laugh at this example of peasants' ignorance about measurement. But we treat modern-day measurements with the same misunderstanding. We confuse the measure with the underlying entity. We eat the menu rather than the meal.

Consider, for example, the economic metric of the *Gross Domestic Product* (GDP). This is the primary economic measure that business and government use to establish financial and social policy for the country. This measure is the sum of all money changing hands that the government can record and count. The assumption underlying the measure is that our economy is healthy when a lot of money changes hands. But there are flaws in this manner of reckoning. These flaws are so serious that some thoughtful economists believe the gross domestic product bears no relationship to the happiness and well-being of the citizenry.[2]

As a riveting example, according to the GDP, one of the most economically productive members of society is someone undergoing treatment for terminal cancer while at the same time going through a divorce. These events cause a lot of money to circulate and boost the gross domestic product. But for the people affected, these events are a catastrophe, not an economic miracle. Generalizing from this example, we can see how a supposedly healthy economy, such as we have today,

---

[2] "If the GDP is Up, Why is America Down?" by C. Cobb, T. Halstead, and J. Rowe, *Atlantic Monthly*, October, 1995, p.59, ff.

can coexist with a depressed and demoralized populace. According to the GDP, hurricanes, earthquakes, crimes, diseases, and wars are all good because of the economic activity they generate. Since the goal of national economic policy is to stimulate the GDP, you might wonder whether the measure and the resulting policies are counterproductive to the well-being of people.

> **The amount of the money measured by the gross domestic product is not meaningful without some consideration of the circumstances that cause money to change hands.**

Where Does Profit Come From?

By analogy to the gross domestic product, consider that ultimate measure of business success, *the bottom line.* One legacy of the Industrial Revolution is the current widespread belief that the primary purpose of business is profit. Profit is clearly necessary. But is it sufficient? Twentieth-century thinking has, at its core, a hidden assumption that effects must have single, or at least primary, causes. It is difficult, from 20th-century perspective, to deal with situations in which multiple causes determine the outcome or where success hinges on the synergistic interaction of many factors.

Consider the case that any business must cater to at least six special interest groups:

customers,

employees,

suppliers,

the community,

government, and

investors.

A business cannot exist without the continued goodwill and cooperation of all of these groups. For example, a business with no customers cannot survive. Similarly, a company that does not heed government regulations or direction will face trouble. A backlash of the reengineering and downsizing trends is that politicians are talking about getting tough with business. The proposals range from cutting *corporate welfare* (special tax breaks) to introducing tax incentives for companies that invest in their workforce and seek to grow business rather than downsize.

The neighbors of a chemical plant in the Northeast organize against the company, in response to constant pollution spills in the neighborhood. They persevere and succeed in shutting the plant down. Another company tries to boost its profits by stretching out payments to suppliers to 120 days, meanwhile dunning customers to pay within 15 days. Eventually, reputable suppliers choose not to deal with the company, and its customers find other vendors.

Interestingly, none of the stakeholders in a company (customers, employees, suppliers, the community, governments, and investors) may see current profits as the fundamental purpose of business. For example, customers want quality goods and services at a fair price. Thus marketing is designed to attract attention to the quality of the goods, not the size of the corporate profits.

Imagine the effect of an advertising campaign that touted a company's "true" purpose. Suppose you develop a telemarketing campaign for a long-distance phone service. The telemarketers' line is:

We're in business for profit, to squeeze every last dime out of you. Sign up, and help our stockholders grow rich.

The campaign would be a disaster. Yet, this is precisely the way some companies speak internally about their customers and their products. For example, one corporate sales force calls themselves hunters and skinners. Hunters find the customers. Skinners flay them. A world-wide credit card company worked hard to come up with this: *Our vision is to gain 100% of the plastic spending of the customers we target.* Many people in the company may be passionate about providing a valuable service to their customers, but this statement more clearly conveys a passion for competition and profit. If this company had the audacity to advertise that they are more concerned about the bottom line than about their customers, their customers would quickly disappear. Therefore, if maximizing profits is indeed the fundamental purpose of business, it is a purpose that business must hide from the customers. Can a purpose that must be hidden be viable in the long run?

If your customers find out that all you care about is profit, they may not remain your customers.

One of the world's largest financial-service firms has recently introduced a new executive pay scheme. The weight given to the executives' performance in handling relationships with the various communities is as follows:

1) return to shareholders - 50%

2) value generated for customers - 25%

3) effective management of employees - 25%

4) contributions to community at large - 0%

5) managing relationships with suppliers - 0%

6) managing relations with the government - 0%

In other words, executive pay is weighted twice as much for generating return for shareholders as for delivering value to customers. Naturally, these weightings do not appear in the company's advertising, which instead gives the impression of a totally customer-oriented company.

Ironically, even investors are not always interested in profits. For example, NetScape Communications, the internet-access software company, had the largest one-day run-up of stock price in history on the day of its initial offering. NetScape, however, had never shown any profits up to the day of its initial public offering. The investors were interested in the possibility of future profits, not past or even current profits. And future profits, of course, depend on how well a business manages its relationships with all its stakeholders: customers, employees, suppliers, the community at large, the government, and the investors.

> Each constituent assesses the value of a company based on the results the constituent is interested in producing.

For example, illegal drug dealers make a great deal of money. The government does not share in the gains since drug dealers rarely declare their earnings. Further, the havoc wreaked on communities and the cost to taxpayers are great. As a consequence, the government and the community want to get rid of drug dealers no matter how much money they make. The four remaining stakeholders (customers, employees, suppliers, and investors), however, have a different view of the drug trade.

Even in business, the context surrounding profit is what determines its true value. This fact leads to the question: *What results are we trying to produce in business?* Specifically, for the people who own and operate the business, what results are they trying to produce? Are those results consonant with the results the stakeholders want?

> Could the 21st-century company be committed to the true best good of all stakeholders?

A vision that says, *Make money!* is not wrong. Profits are necessary, but not sufficient, to get the best from people. For example, it is often difficult for individuals in large corporations to maintain a sense of the value of their work and whether it makes a difference to anyone. Great companies take steps to identify and share the significance of their work, in addition to its profitability.

> **A malaise and lack of leadership among employees may arise from their disconnection with any sense of contributing to the community.**

Another result of the drive to ever-greater profits is the legislation that has grown up to protect workers. Most of the legislation is the result of efforts by the labor movement on behalf of the workers. Laws that we take for granted such as regulations regarding workers compensation, paid vacations, the five-day work week, and pension plans come from union actions. These laws have made a powerful contribution to the humane treatment of workers. Yet legislating corporate behavior is a two-sided sword. Such legislation can become both the reason and the justification for company treatment of employees. Companies are able to say, *We do thus and such because the laws require us to do so. Where the law makes no requirement, we do whatever is financially expedient. After all, we are in business to make money.* Companies are then relieved from asking themselves, *What is the value we place on our employees? How should we treat our workers?*

> **Personal responsibility for the treatment of people is lost when everyone, worker and corporation alike, says, *I work solely to make money.***

Together, employer and employee create the context of the company. Success in the 21st century requires thoughtful action for the true best good of *all* stakeholders: customers, investors, suppliers, the community at large, employees, and the government. An appropriate question for the 21st-century thinker is:

What context will generate both profits and prosperity?

CONSUMERISM AND WORK ADDICTION

Getting and Spending

The preoccupation of business with profits is analogous to the preoccupation of jobholders with a paycheck. When profits become an end in themselves they mask other business values. When the paycheck becomes an end in itself, people deny themselves much of what life has to offer. There are many possible reasons to work including love for what you do, camaraderie, intellectual stimulation, and the opportunity to create something of value. When people limit their reason for working to a paycheck, they hold themselves back, not wanting to put in more than the job is worth. But the reasons to throw yourself into your work are never related to money.

Through history, regular pay was never a part of work until the Industrial Revolution. The invention of regular jobs brings regular pay. There is a steady influx of cash into an economy that previously was cash-poor. In an agrarian economy, families raise their food and naturally recycle their possessions wherever possible. So, for example, flour sacks become towels and worn clothing becomes quilts. The consistent availability of cash changes this world into the consumer society we know today. An industrial society forms a self-fulfilling system for consumerism. Goods are available in massive quantities and the jobs producing those goods yield the cash to buy them. The consumption cycle is not good or bad, simply self-contained. It is also hypnotic. One typical professional couple spends their Saturdays engaged in mad shopping sprees after which they cart all of their new possessions home, unboxing and assembling them. In the evening they haul their discardables down the stairs of their split-level home to the garage and load them into the mini van for a trip to the town dump on Sunday. One day they have powerful insight into their own buying habits. *Our home is a processing plant for consumer goods!* they realize. This realization is the seed for alternative, less addictive, and more fun ways to invest their precious weekends as well as their money.

Such insight is rare. Consumerism is built on the premises of dissatisfaction and never-enough.

> **Money enables people who are miserable on the job to spend evenings and weekends in the mindless respite of spending.**

Unfortunately, mindless spending reinforces the belief that people *really need the money* and cannot possibly afford to leave their jobs to do something they might really love.

Consider Lynn, a woman of many talents, who loves reading, writing, editing, and publishing. After spending years as a technical writer for a mega-corporation, she purchases a small copyediting business with the idea of building her own company. She and her husband are both professionals and, with their children gone, have come to enjoy a high material standard of living. So although self-employment is what she has always dreamed about, Lynn cannot bring herself to leave her corporate job. She believes she needs her paycheck to make the mortgage payment. Never mind that she is miserable at work and too exhausted at night to make a go of the new business. After a year of running her fledgling company on the side, she faces the dilemma of whether to sell it while it is still afloat or to continue to fund its operation out of her income. Of course, the deteriorating financial picture in her business makes it ever more daunting to leave the regular income of the corporate world.

> **The cycle of earn-and-spend reinforces an addictive dependency on a regular paycheck.**

Consumerism is a thoughtless and egocentric way of living that masks our separation from others. For example, Susan is a director for a financial services corporation. She is addicted to the bonuses, the expensive clothing, and lavish vacations. When she leaves the company to start her own business, it is with tremendous apprehension. What occurs is a great shock. For the first time in her life she knows that her work is actually helping people and she is ecstatic. Focused on her new business, she has neither the money nor the interest to spend and simply stops. Shopping becomes a purposeful activity rather than recreation. Recreation becomes gardening and hiking and reading. Even when Susan begins making more money than ever, she uses her income differently than before.

Workaholism

All of us work long hours at some time in our careers, perhaps due to a crisis or a crucial project. If work is a labor of love you may spend hours lost to the outside world. These are not symptoms of workaholism.

> **Workaholism is giving in to the long-term habit of working extensive hours from a sense of duty or obligation or from the need to gain approval or success.**

Workaholism is a common 20th-century addiction. The greatest difficulty with this disease is that many companies reward and encourage it. Even when employees know that working long hours does not enhance the quality of their results, they fall prey to the pressure to demonstrate their dedication. Often, having too much work to do is considered a sign of importance and *being in demand*. In many companies, employees are proud to be considered workaholics.

> Workaholism is an addiction that often hides from people their enormous dissatisfaction with their work.

Studies have shown that the most common reason workaholics refuse to take vacations is that they hate to come back to work. Apparently the misery of returning is so great they prefer not to leave in the first place. What must work be like for such a person? Let us look at Paul's situation.

Paul is a corporate manager. While not unhappy, he is certainly uninspired by his work. For years his approach has been to do what is expected of him, not make waves, and get the paperwork in on time. What he really enjoys about his job are the bonuses, the stock options, the expense account, the business travel, the private office, the secretary and the covered parking. In short, Paul stays with his job for the perks, the *golden handcuffs* of business lore. The content of his work holds no excitement for him. Nonetheless he works hard, is extremely busy, often works into the evening, and comes to the office on weekends. Feeling overworked is his primary reassurance of his value to the company. He does not otherwise have a personal vision of the value of his work. When the organization announces a far-reaching overhaul, Paul senses the likelihood of being laid off. At first this petrifies him but, even before his last day, he senses growing excitement. The new and the unknown beckon him. After all, he has never worked anywhere else in over 30 years of employment. What is the outside like? What will a different job be like? Could it even be fun?

Paul is not so rare among middle managers in corporate America. Perhaps his job beat him down over the years. Maybe he never belonged in the job in the first place. Whatever the case, he has no passion for management nor for any aspect of his job as he understands it. Workaholism helps us to ignore that we are not doing work that we love.

The layoff may be the best possible turn of events for Paul. If he takes advantage of this opportunity to reconsider what is his rightful work, he may land a job he truly loves.

> **If people refused to stay where they have no passion, would there be a need for radical reengineering in companies?**

The cost of *not* changing when either opportunity or crisis strikes can be high. Following all the corporate rules, by 1985 Mark rises to group manager in charge of 100 people. He says *Yes, Sir* to his boss and tries to make the message palatable to his troops. One day, he gets the offer to be manager of Research, a job that is his true dream. Mark is at heart a visionary. But he frets that the research job will divert him from the corporate ladder, the so-called line positions where you control real budgets for real products. So he turns his dream job down and figures to make it someday as a major corporate bigshot, or at least survive as a minor bigshot.

Fast forward to 1993. In a single day, Mark is laid off, his wife leaves him, and he cuts off the tips of his fingers trying to distract himself in his expensive woodworking shop. Picking himself up from these disasters, what does he do? Go back to his true dream? No, he sends out hundreds of resumes for another line position, eventually landing a job as vice-president in a second-rate company. A year later, he is laid off again when the company disbands his entire division.

IS THERE A BETTER WAY TO WORK?

Many people are experiencing the pain of transition, not just in their jobs and careers, but in the rules of the workplace itself. Many companies are in a time of transition, struggling to be competitive, deciding what work to do in-house, what work to outsource, what business to be in, and how to treat all the different groups on whom their existence and prosperity depend. Could it be that these uncertainties actually hold great promise? As with any major change, the end of the traditional workplace invites us to examine afresh our deeply rooted assumptions about life, time, and money. New answers may be far more satisfying and productive than the workplace culture, norms, and solutions the 20th century provided.

Some economists are predicting that it will take 50 years for the new workplace to emerge. In the meantime, many of our largest corporations will vanish. Not just jobs, but entire areas of endeavor will disappear. In other fields, wage and salary scales will be cut in half. We face 50 years of uncertainty, say the economists.

Consider a different view. Economic projections extrapolate present trends and treat people as passive statistics. Economic theory does not take into account the one thing, the only thing, that can change the future—*you*. You as an individual creating the next century using radically new ideas and approaches. *You* inventing products, services, and ways of making a living no one has even dreamed of yet. *You* proactively leading your company in a new direction, not just reacting to trends. You having the courage to step outside the known. The rest of this book shows a way of thinking and a set of tools designed for the 21st century.

3

Could Work Be Wonderful?

I don't like work—no man does—but I like what is in work—the
chance to find yourself. Your own reality—for yourself, not for others—
what no other man can ever know.

. . . JOSEPH CONRAD, *Heart of Darkness*

In the previous chapter, we saw some of the difficulties that individuals
and companies are experiencing as the 20th century draws to a close. A
common denominator for these difficulties may be the perspective from
which the people involved are viewing the purpose and the possible rewards of work. In the examples we give, for companies the focus is profits above all other ends. For employees, the parallel focus is on a
predictable paycheck, above all else.

This chapter gives examples of companies and individuals who have
found another way. Though all unique, each individual and each company
whose story we present have certain things in common. All are successful
by ordinary business standards—the companies are profitable and the individuals make a good living. Beyond that, they all take a broader perspective on work than just profits and pay. They expect more from work,
and they get it. They defy conventional wisdom and standard advice,

choosing instead to create, through words and deeds, the world of work they would like to live in.

COULD WORK BE ITS OWN REWARD?

An undercover narcotics officer takes a bullet in a routine drug raid. It warrants a small article in the local newspaper and few of the citizens take notice. He is lucky to be alive and finds himself forced into disability retirement. Nonetheless, he feels like he is embarking on a dream vacation when he moves his family to Arizona. At first he enjoys the leisurely lifestyle but within a few months becomes discontented and begins to yearn for his old job. He misses his friends and the camaraderie that comes from facing challenges together. He decides to go back to work and ultimately lands a position as a security guard for a large company. His job lacks the thrill of drug enforcement work and consists mostly of checking badges at the employees' entrance. But he is delighted to experience again the friendships, the discipline, and the meaning of work. Less than a year later, his wife purchases a state lottery ticket and they win $3,400,000. This man, who has given up his disability retirement for the love of work, is now presented with the opportunity to retire as a wealthy man. He considers the possibility but has learned too much to quit. There is vagary to retirement and value in work. After a brief and glamorous vacation, he is back in uniform, checking badges.

What about you? If you win the lottery will you quit working? Do you think you work just to pay the mortgage or to cover the college tuition for your children? Many people who win the lottery leave their jobs only to return. What are they thinking, these repatriates to the workaday world that was once so onerous? Where there was seemingly no choice, now there is no reason, outside of themselves, to endure the discipline of a job.

> Is it possible that once the burden of having to work is removed, you would discover motives sufficiently strong to warrant choosing to work?

Many people feel forced to work because they need the money. This *feeling* is misunderstood as the *reason* that they work. Nothing could be further from the truth.

Perhaps work is not just about getting paid. Much valuable and crucial work is not paid at all. Consider child bearing, visiting the sick, ticket-taking for the Little Theater, or picking up litter on a public street. Many entrancing hobbies, such as gardening, cooking, or re-building an old car, bear a striking similarity to work. Many people of great personal wealth work non-stop, organizing fund raising and volunteering time to their communities. We consider it an insult to say, *That person will do anything for a buck.* Yet, that is exactly what you are doing if you will not consider leaving a miserable job that pays well for one that is far more satisfying yet pays poorly. Underemployment, creative or financial, is the plight of many workers today, workers who are deluded into thinking that they do, indeed, work for money.

Alyssia is Director of Sales for high-tech products and makes a great deal of money working for an industry-leading firm. Time and again her total commitment to helping her customers solve problems wins her yet another sale. But her joy in work has diminished over the last few years. The company has grown dramatically, due in large measure to her contribution. Now she feels that people have become numbers, that she no longer knows everyone in the company, and her firm is being bought out by an even larger organization. When she examines her personal motivation for working, she discovers, *Ever since my husband walked out and left me with a baby I have worked in a frenzy of fear to put food on the table. It may seem humorous now that my daughter is 23 and I have a comfortable lifestyle, but this fear still drives me.* Alyssia sees that although her motive for working has been fear of starvation, she really loves her occupation because she loves her co-workers and her customers. She thrives on the warm and personal relationships built over many years. A short time later she leaves her prestigious employer for an opportunity with old and dear friends in a risky start-up business.

> When the context and our true motives for working are clarified, we are able to create a work environment that more accurately reflects our true purpose.

COULD WORK BE GRATIFYING?

Some people have found a way to work that resonates with and supports deeply held personal values. *God makes the wheat berry unique every season and in every region. When God is finished, our work begins and we produce a high-quality and consistent flour for our bakeries.* Can you hear the love of this manager for his work? He is responsible for the world's largest soft-wheat flour mill and it would be easy for him to spend all of his time overseeing the plant operations. While management demands most of his time, each year he reserves a few precious days for himself to visit the local farms. He speaks with the farmers and takes samples of the season's wheat berries before harvest. Those samples remain displayed on his desk until the next season. The bowls of wheat berries are a tangible reminder of why he got into the business of making flour.

In school districts across the nation, bus drivers pick up children in the morning and get them home safely each day. It is not an easy job. There are medically fragile students to assist and violent children to restrain. Angry motorists, resentful at waiting for the school bus to load or unload, sometimes make obscene gestures or brandish firearms. The drivers see children who are sad, suffering and poor. They have been known to use their own funds to buy mittens, hats, and even coats for the children who have none. Would you do this for $10 an hour? Many school bus drivers do, and they do it with love.

A woman in Colorado Springs makes a large investment by adding a commercial kitchen to her home and acquires the licensing necessary to bake bread for sale. She does not need the money; it is her contribution to the world. In her words, *I consider my love for people to be an ingredient as important as any other. Everyone who eats my bread receives my blessing.*

If you love your work, everyone benefits.

An engineer spends most of his day composing computer code on a terminal. He laughs when he tells that his small son thinks his dad's work consists of typing. To the literal eye of his son, the job is superficial; to the man, his joy is deeper seated. He is fully absorbed and dedicated to his labor. Even knowing that his accomplishments will disappear as technology moves on and changes makes no difference. A skilled laborer who forgets himself as he focuses on the task at hand is similar to the engineer. It may seem ironic that, when we are lost in our work, we are most at peace and fully alive.

What makes work satisfying? Does doing what we love have anything to do with it? One man believes in the magic of making cereal. He is a manager at a cereal plant, and although he does not say so, he revels in the opportunity to give visitors a tour. He explains how the product is made, its movement through massive ducts from the cookers to the gun room and on to the packaging lines. His visitors peer through thick glass windows to watch the cereal explode from guns that fill a thirty-foot room. He encourages them to climb scaffolding and see the multi-million-dollar scales that package exactly the right amount of product in each size box. His eyes twinkle behind his safety glasses and he has the look of a child climbing over the biggest toys he has ever found.

Work is joyful when we are able to do what we love, to produce what others see as valuable.

Norm Winningstad is one of the richest men in the Pacific Northwest. He has founded a dozen firms, including Floating Point Systems and Lattice Semiconductors. An employee once asked him, *Norm, what do you do when you don't have to do anything?* Here is his unforgettable reply: *It depends on why you did it in the first place. If you work hard so you can stop working, then you stop working…instantly. But if you worked for the joy of creation and the fun of collaboration, then a ton of money doesn't change anything. Well, maybe the money allows you to do even more.*

COULD WORK GENERATE SELF-WORTH?

A director for a Fortune 50 travel company has his position eliminated as a result of reengineering. He is given a temporary position heading a department that will be eliminated within a year. His job is to oversee the short-term group, turn the work over to another department, and fire the employees. He has misgivings about his position. In the tradition of lame-duck managers, he receives little encouragement and no acknowledgment. Even at a distance, it is clear that he is unhappy and feels betrayed. Shortly before the end of the year, he finds another job. But this job involves contributing, not destroying. He is now the training and quality manager for the business travel division with responsibility to insure that his people know and serve their customers' needs. When his friends see him at the gym after he lands the new position, they do not need to ask how it is going because of the amazing alteration in his appearance. It is as though this middle-aged man is a confident and lanky kid again, eyes and smile filled with innocent yet determined promise. *They make it clear they really need me and I'm building something*, he says with enthusiasm.

> When we cannot see our results, or are unsure of their contribution to anyone, our work becomes dispirited and meaningless. Conversely, work that is appreciated takes on new meaning and vibrancy.

Tony Farias comes from Argentina. He works as a custodian for several companies. He moonlights as a carpenter, which was his trade in Argentina. All this work lets him send money back to his less fortunate relatives in Argentina and visit them every several years. When you meet Tony, you sense integrity and purpose. If you hire him to build some shelves or cabinets in your home, you get craftsmanship and care better than any you have ever seen. Tony cleans his customers' bathrooms and offices with the same care. Tony knows why he works, expresses quality in everything he does, and he has a plan. His dream of a home of his own, college for his kids, and comfort for his parents will, without question, come to pass. In the meantime, Tony is a happy man.

COULD WE TAKE PRIDE IN OUR PRODUCTS?

At the Wheat Montana Farm outside Boise, they raise red and white hard wheat pesticide-free on 7,000 acres. The farm is not large by commercial standards nor are the profit margins great. Yet, annually, at harvest, the Wheat Montana Farm engages in a baking contest with several British farms. The goal is to set the world's fastest record for turning standing wheat into a loaf of bread on the table. To do this the farm workers erect a tent within 10 feet of where the grain is harvested. They haul in electrical generators and set up grain grinders and mixers. They hook up a dozen microwave ovens. A crowd of cheerful and unruly onlookers gathers. When the stopwatch starts, the combine driver takes off and cuts just enough wheat for 13 loaves of bread. An employee grabs the bucket of grain and sprints to the tent where the grain is weighed and ground into flour. The mixers beat the ingredients into dough, hand-shape 13 loaves, and race the pans to the ovens. Just a few minutes later the bakers remove the bread and, when the last loaf hits the table, the referee stops the clock. The world record, held by the Wheat Montana Farm, is 8 minutes and 13 seconds to produce a loaf of bread and the contestants are brainstorming to produce a four-minute loaf. The question is why. Perhaps for fun as much as for profit.

Gil LaPorte is a builder of houses. In the 1980s he prospers, building the custom houses and additions he loves. Two-by-eight-inch floor joists satisfy the building code, but result in squeaks and floors that bounce when you jump on them. Gil likes to use 2-by-12-inch joists, which are costlier but give a truly solid floor. Then, in the late 1980s, the housing market tanks and people cannot afford 2-by-12-inch floor joists. Let alone solid floor joists, buyers cannot even afford houses with closets. Gil could stay in business making houses with no closets, but chooses not to: *I just can't build a house that will be inadequate for people down the road*, he says. So instead, he works in an auto junkyard during the late eighties and brings his characteristic enthusiasm and eye for quality. The junkyard thrives and Gil makes more than he ever made building houses. But when the housing market recovers in the early nineties, Gil goes back to the custom building he really loves. These transitions do not bother him at all. He revels in them as part of the game of the working life.

Two entrepreneurs love golf. They invent a rubberized substance that makes an ideal material for golf club grips. To promote their new product, they visit professional golf tournaments, offering to install their new grips on the pro's clubs and to replace the originals at the end of the round if the pros are not delighted. Their enthusiasm and their free offer persuade many pros to give the new product a try. Most become enthusiastic spokespeople and the new company succeeds.

Of all life's satisfactions, a job well done ranks pretty high.

Terrance is a third generation New England stonemason. A master craftsman, he builds with brick, but what he loves most is making stone walls. His love of stone has enabled him to buy 20 acres and a home that would otherwise be unaffordable. His 20 acres, which perhaps only he could love, is a huge field of stones from which he takes what he needs for his business, saving the best pieces for his house.

Apple Computer boasts an incredible run of success. Started in a garage, the company went on to become one of the most revered brand names in history, with unsurpassed loyalty among its customers. So deep is this reservoir of customer loyalty that it today gives Apple every chance to survive a decade of missed opportunities and unfortunate management decisions. Its core early product, the Macintosh computer, propelled the company to more than a decade of success without further fundamental innovation. Did you know that inside the cover of early Macintosh models, molded into the plastic, are the signatures of the design team that created it?

COULD SMALL BE SUCCESSFUL?

Some, perhaps most, companies upon which our abundant way of life depends do not have growth as a goal. These companies are driven by other values, such as longevity or being a valued member of an ongoing community. This can be most easily seen in small companies that continue to be owned and operated by the founders. Owners of some of these companies are entrepreneurs whose driving motivation is growth. But most of them are businesses that will never grow, by the express desire of the owner. One such business owner has his company situated in the rolling Connecticut countryside. He is an engineer who designs a specialty high-pressure valve for utility companies. The valve is far better than anything else available on the market and his business flourishes, growing to almost 100 employees and 10 million dollars in annual sales. Then, without fanfare, this privately held firm stops growing. The owner has reached the limits of his own capability to run the company and he does not wish to turn the company over to someone else. Decades pass and he remains just as passionate about his company as the day he began. His children pursue other careers and, as he approaches retirement, he brings new managers into the firm. Though people sometimes pressure him to take advantage of a booming market to grow the company, he politely ignores their advice. What drives the owner is a love of the business and not a desire for more power or money.

COULD EMPLOYEES' SKILLS BE FULLY UTILIZED?

Traditionally, we hire a person for a defined job. We define the requirements, seek the person who best fulfills those requirements, and expect the job, as we have defined it, to be done. This may be a consequence of 20th-century thinking that equates people with machines. Just as each machine is designed with exactly one purpose, 20th-century thinking about women and men applies the same standard. A worker is trained for specific duties. If the duties are eliminated, so too is the person. He is not assumed capable of an alternate function. Even the worker has been hypnotized to disbelieve in his own capabilities.

When a company buys (hires) a human being, however, it purchases something entirely different from a machine. A human being is not just a specific set of fixed skills, but also the only entity in existence that exhibits creativity and can generate better ideas about how best to run the business it was hired to support.

> Twenty-first-century thinking holds that people can grow, change, and create.

Elaine is a secretary in a large corporation. Her job description says that she is supposed to type correspondence, answer the phone, set up meetings, and arrange travel. But when Elaine learns word processing, she becomes enthralled with computers. On her own initiative, she learns graphics and presentation software. Soon, she is preparing slide presentations for her boss. Word spreads, and Elaine is in great demand. Managers who used to stay late preparing their presentations now leave it to Elaine, knowing their presentation slides will be perfect. Elaine gets no tangible reward for this work—no raises and no promotion—because nothing in the job descriptions and classifications allow for rewarding a secretary as one would a graphic designer. The company is getting an incredible bargain. Hiring someone versed in presentation software who also has an eye for graphic design would cost two to three times Elaine's salary. But Elaine does it because she wants to, and she enjoys being appreciated and valued.

At a manufacturing plant, one of the union stewards is a natural facilitator and supporter for people. She is known for being outspoken and adamant that people should work hard, work together, and get the job done. When the company is ready to automate several lines, far from being even considered for lay-off, she is asked to become a trainer for the new work processes. Her commonsense approach to the work systems and her high expectations for her own performance as well as the performances of her co-workers make her a natural choice for the training role.

Titles and job descriptions obscure the full range of contributions that individuals are able to make.

Consider a corporate manager who is especially gifted at coaching and grooming new managers. His peers would like to ask him for advice but will not do so. The people who could use his help fear that asking him will be interpreted by their managers as a sign that he should be promoted over them. Rather than risk the appearance of vulnerability, they choose to continue with the management styles they already understand. Ultimately, this man leaves his job and becomes a highly paid consultant providing personal coaching for top executives, the same service his colleagues would not dare accept for free.

According to the WALL STREET JOURNAL, John Deere, a manufacturer of agricultural equipment, has on its payroll a thinker who dabbles in an esoteric branch of mathematics called chaos theory.[1] He is an anomaly in the midst of a production-oriented world. Fortunately for the company, this man is given the freedom to delve into new ideas and one day he sees a connection between chaos theory and manufacturing processes. This allows him, with the help of others, to invent a new approach to production scheduling that saves John Deere tens of millions of dollars in production costs.

We think and speak about work as action. *What do you do? What are you doing now? What do you want to do when you grow up?* Yet, what commends us in our jobs is seldom related to the specifics of doing. More important is the being, *who* and *how* we *are* at work. The most sought-after characteristics in job interviews are a positive attitude, self-motivation, and the ability to work as a member of a team. These are

---

[1]"At Deere They Know a Mad Scientist may be a Firm's Biggest Asset," by Tom Petzinger, Jr., *Wall Street Journal*, July 14, 1995.

characteristics of *being* ourselves. Consider Mike, a technical advisor for the computer systems in a large corporation. You might think his value to his company lies in his extensive and detailed technical knowledge. But in a mere 15 years with his employer he has mastered three radically new technologies. His work today utilizes none of the skills for which he was hired and none of the skills he used even five years ago. His value lies in his never-ending interest in learning, his willingness to experiment with new ideas, and most of all, his zeal to see automation simplify work for others.

> Rather than eliminate the worker, why not rethink how to use the worker's talents?

COULD INTERPERSONAL SKILLS CREATE PROFITS?

One larger-than-life entrepreneur has amassed a net worth of twenty million dollars at age 32 by using his communication skills. His game is buying and selling businesses. Much like people who search out houses to fix up and resell, he finds businesses, fixes them up and flips them a year later for a high margin of profit. What's intriguing to watch is his mastery of interpersonal communications. His requests and promises are always bold, outrageous, and come from nothing. The velocity at which he generates results is amazing. First, he makes sure that what he is offering or selling is sufficiently attractive. He is always listening for the customer's commitment to buy and imposes a high level of discipline on the process to secure that commitment by using specific deadlines and nonrefundable financial deposits. He requests a high level of intentionality from the buyer and that they act expeditiously. He listens intently for what the customer wants out of the deal and invents unforeseen but appropriate structures accordingly. He keeps his word and demands that the people he deals with keep theirs.

A major division of a Fortune 50 company reorganizes its management structure. The intent is to move from hierarchical management to a self-empowered team approach. One hundred and nineteen middle managers lose their old jobs. Of these only 24 are invited to stay under the new system. The reason? The people invited to stay have the best interpersonal skills, especially in the area of supporting others.

COULD WORK BE INTEGRATED WITH LIFE?

Native Americans do not have words for *work* or *job*. There is only the activity of living that includes whatever is needed to feed and clothe the people. Without work, there is no *unemployment*. Nor is there a word for *late*. These are 20th-century concepts. Twenty-first century ideas let us consider alternative work practices.

I can and do work at any hour of the day or night. Wherever and whenever I am needed. These are the words of a successful management consultant. But, he also admits that when he is in his (home) office, his hours are not the typical corporate schedule of 9 to 5, Monday through Friday. He wakes up with the sun, loves to work in his pajamas until noon and is just as likely to work Saturday and take Tuesday off. *At first I was really concerned about self-discipline and I was careful to work all day everyday. I was confused about the weekends, too. Had I worked hard enough to deserve the weekend off? And, why is the weekend always Saturday and Sunday?* This independently-employed man has earned a new relationship with himself through his freedom at work. He discovers a natural discipline in his way of working and an overarching rhythm to his life.

COULD THE WORKPLACE BE A COMMUNITY?

Warren Rosenfeld, CEO of Cal Bag, does not fit the mold of a profit-driven businessman. He explains that Cal Bag, a refuse-processing company, is a third generation business, started by his grandfather who emigrated from Russia. His business mission is startlingly simple. *Our goal is longevity. Our game plan is driven by loyalty—loyal customers and loyal employees. We believe that employee stability is the key to long-term growth.* Cal Bag has almost no employee turnover. Rosenfeld says that the company's best partners are local government agencies who assist them in navigating the maze of waste disposal and environmental protection laws and who work with the company to maintain a healthy relationship with the community.[1]

We do not exist outside of the community that gives us meaning.

Work makes us fully a member of the community of woman and man. Work says we belong. To work at something you love will change your life. To have no work will destroy your life. Work is also about the future. We want to make a contribution that will live after we are gone. At one wonderful factory in the South, a gilded plaque in the entrance honors, with brass nameplate, every employee who ever retired from the plant. This says to every employee *I'm part of something important, something with tradition, purpose, and a future. It means something to work here.*

COULD YOUR WORK LIVE ON AFTER YOU ARE GONE?

Digital Equipment Corporation is recovering after losing half of its employees. CEO Robert Palmer is making profitable deals with Microsoft. The key bargaining card in these deals is the 64-bit Alpha microprocessor chip. Alpha would not exist but for the determined efforts of many people, but chief among these is Peter Conklin, the recently deceased Alpha program manager. Three years before his death, Peter makes a public vow that each contribution he will henceforth make to his company would be worth twice the value of the previous contribution. He

---

[1]Marketplace, National Public Radio, April 8, 1996.

has no idea how to do this, but proceeds anyway on raw courage and determination. His last and only project after his bold declaration is Alpha and, although he never lives to see its fruition, it is, to anyone who knows, his legacy and the fulfillment of his impossible commitment.

> At some time in your life, you may come to the realization that what you have to contribute to the world is more important than even your physical existence.

COULD MANAGEMENT BE NOBLE?

Consider the case of Malden Mills, one of the last great textile mills in New England. Just before Christmas 1995, an explosion injures 33 workers and destroys three of the factory's century-old red-brick buildings. Amid smoking piles of twisted metal and debris, mill owner Aaron Fuerstein makes an incredible announcement: *With God's help we will overcome the events of the past 12 hours and continue to be a vital force in New England.* A few days later he announces that employees will receive full pay while the plant is rebuilt. *People thought I did such a saintly thing. I did a normal thing,* he explains, and talks about a time when it was only natural for a company owner, if disaster struck, to rebuild, worry about his workers, and begin again in the same community.

Harley-Davidson is another company that believes *in doing what's right for someone other than just yourself.* In the words of Richard Teerlink,[2] the CEO, *Today we could increase our prices dramatically and sell every motorcycle we manufacture. But we have opted to price our product at or less than inflation (for price increases) even though the market would willingly pay dramatically higher prices and all that money would go down to the*

---

[2]Marketplace, National Public Radio, March 12, 1996.

CHESTER COLLEGE LIBRARY

bottom line. But we think it is not fair to those loyal customers who were with us when we didn't know if we were going to make it back in the early 80's.

COULD ANY OF THIS WORK FOR YOU?

Twentieth-century thinking leads us to focus on work as a means to a limited end, either profits or paycheck. But to take this perspective robs work of most of its possibilities. Both profits and paychecks are means to greater ends. To focus on either exclusively, as an end in itself, is self-defeating. Twenty-first-century thinking—which harks back to an old and noble idea of work—takes an expansive view.

You do not work just for a paycheck. You are not in business just for profit. Life has too much more to offer.

Perhaps you have seen some possibilities for yourself or for your company in these stories of people who have found their way. All are in some sense ordinary, not the once-in-a-generation Andrew Carnegies or Bill Gateses of this world. A rich and satisfying worklife is everyone's birthright.

What if the true possibility of business is a world that works for everyone?

Part II

A Better Way to Work

To think that you can go in five different directions tomorrow and succeed makes you totally unafraid of losing what you have today.
. . . JOAN LUNDEN, Co-host of *Good Morning America*

4

The Power of Perspectives

Because we are unaccustomed to it, we don't usually see that there's a third possible logical term equal to yes and no which is capable of expanding our understanding in an unrecognized direction. We don't even have a term for it, so I'll have to use the Japanese *mu*.

Mu ...states that the context of the question is such that a yes or no answer is an error and should not be given. "Unask the question" is what it says.

Mu becomes appropriate when the context of the question becomes too small for the truth of the answer.

. . . ROBERT PIRISG, *Zen and the Art of Motorcycle Maintenance*

HOW TO GET THE MOST FROM THIS CHAPTER

Usually, we take action to solve our problems. This chapter, and the next two, show another—more powerful—method. Problems always exist against some background of assumptions. You can take the 20th-century approach of attacking the problem directly, but often the 21st-century alternative of rethinking the background, the perspective, the assumptions that have the problem be a problem in the first place, will give you better results.

The ideas in this chapter will be of most value if you relate them to specific issues in your worklife where you would like to see improvement. Make a note of at least one answer to each of the following questions, and keep the list in front of you as you read. When you come across an example or an idea in the chapter that gives you an insight or new way of looking at your issue, write it down.

- Identify at least one area in your professional or personal life where you are not satisfied with the results you are achieving. Be specific.
- Make note of an unresolved conflict, professional or personal, in which you are currently involved.
- Think of a project or task where you are trying to introduce change in your work or personal life, but where the people affected are resisting.

THE WORLD OF RIGHT AND WRONG

One common 20th-century assumption is that there is a right and a wrong to every situation. This way of approaching problems has profound consequences. In this section we present four scenarios of conflict where issues of right and wrong figure heavily. As you read, notice whether you remain detached from each scenario or whether you tend to take one side or the other. The section then gives tools for approaching right-versus-wrong issues that can give better results. If you keep your own issues in mind as you read, you are likely to have ideas for new, more powerful actions to take.

A Neighborhood at Odds

A young couple, thrilled to have realized the American dream of owning a home, moves into the neighborhood. They have scraped together what capital they can for the down payment and made the best possible purchase they could find for their money. A few months after moving in, they paint the exterior of the house lime green. This is an unusual choice in staid New England where house colors typically range from gray to white, or sometimes barn red.

The neighbors are incredulous and incensed. Ringleaders draft a petition which they carry around the subdivision for signatures, demanding the house be immediately repainted. A delegation of irate residents delivers the petition to the homeowners and expresses their anger. You can imagine the reaction of the young couple. They are shocked and then outraged and order their insulting neighbors to get off their property. The standoff goes on for months, eventually years, with neighbors taking one side or the other. All of this tears apart the community with a high cost in resentment and animosity not to mention courtesies never extended and friendships never formed.

You can, perhaps, identify with this scenario. The neighbors are worried about an eyesore and a decline in property values. Will they be able to sell their homes easily if the subdivision is deemed tawdry? What will the homeowners do next? Will they install an old car on cement blocks in the front yard? As for the young couple, you can assume they did not pull together every penny of cash and undertake a 30-year mortgage just to watch the investment swirl down the drain. They certainly intended the best and may have considered the color an improvement in the neighborhood.

- ♦ Who is right?
- ♦ Do the neighbors have the right to protect their interests?
- ♦ Does the young couple have the right to do as they please with their home?

Hostility on the Job

Consider another true story. This one is about working people, management and union, in a manufacturing plant. The workforce is organized and has been since the plant opened 50 years ago. The plant is in the rust belt, home to the steel industry and to unions with a reputation for hostility and unwillingness to cooperate with management. This plant runs true to form. A strike in the late 50's went on for 10 weeks before the employees settled for a one-penny raise. With this history, it is not surprising that the employees carry grudges.

Today, the management is concerned about the future viability of the plant. The managers see the employees as unwilling to consider even the smallest work changes. The costs are high; equipment and work systems are obsolete. Visitors from other, nonunion plants tell stories of workers and management collaborating effectively and make snide contrasts with this plant. Management characterizes the union committee chairman as a *war devil* who attempts to stymie positive change in a barrage of grievances. The management team thinks that only a painful event can bring any changes. It looks as though the painful event is about to happen. For the plant to remain viable, the company must invest heavily in automation, a move that could eliminate as many as 60% of the production line jobs.

Unlike the managers, most of the union members have a long family and personal history with the plant. The committee chairman says, *If I had a role in keeping this plant alive, it would be the thrill of my life. I want this plant here for my lifetime and for the lifetimes of my children and grandchildren, so a lot of people can earn a good living.* The employees are clearly committed to do whatever is needed to keep the plant open. But they do not believe the managers are concerned about anyone other than themselves and their management careers.

- ♦ Who do you think has the best interests of the plant at heart?
- ♦ Who has the most to lose?
- ♦ Who has the expertise to ensure the plant is competitive?

The Cat in the Sack

Four teenaged boys from Texas torture and kill a stray cat. First they put the cat in a burlap sack and beat on the sack with baseball bats. When the cat is half dead, they drive over the sack with their pick-up truck. The news media picks up the story, which briefly makes national headlines.

The teenagers' actions become known and controversial throughout Texas and divide the community. One group of citizens says that the youths are hooligans, embarked on a path that will end in their becoming sadists and murderers. This camp favors the harshest possible punishment for them. The school principal has already thrown the boys off the baseball team for their actions. If prosecuted under the laws concerning cruelty to animals, they could face up to a year in jail.

The other group of citizens says that the youths were just doing normal Saturday night pranks and that the whole incident should be ignored. This camp is pressuring the principal to reinstate the boys on the baseball team, a move the principal is considering. Furthermore, these citizens are adamant that the boys not face criminal prosecution.

- ◆ Who is right and who is wrong?
- ◆ Should the boys be reinstated, or prosecuted?
- ◆ What is the basis of your judgment?

A Case of Reengineering

Many large companies maintain their own computer and data-processing divisions, although recently there is an increasing trend to outsource these functions. At one large financial services company, the data-processing function has grown for years, peopled with college-educated, technically oriented staff. Over time, the most technically excellent have been promoted to management positions to run the division.

During the years, the managers become accustomed to their positions and a comfortable, familiar way of doing things. Suddenly in the early 1990s a wave of reengineering fever hits. Top executives from corporate headquarters wish to change the management style from an authoritarian, hierarchical approach to an approach with greater collaboration and inclusion of the technical staff in decision making. To make this change happen the executives introduce an entire curriculum of state-of-the-art leadership training and involve the division in an intensive period of management education. But two years later, little has changed. As a new approach, corporate hires a new director for the data-processing division. Beginning with the vice presidents who report to him, the new man quickly eliminates 75 percent of the existing hierarchy and streamlines, strips, replaces, and hires. Many of the individuals who are fired have never worked for another company and are totally unprepared to look for other employment. The employees, especially the managers who remain, are stunned and spend months in gradual recovery from the drastic changes.

- ◆ Was this the right thing to do?
- ◆ Who was responsible for the downfall of the organization?
- ◆ What should be done now?

Which Side Are You on?

Is everyone right? Or is no one right? Is it a matter of different perspectives? One group has one set of interests and another group has a conflicting set of interests. You may be able to see both sides, that is, unless one of these cases triggers something relating to your core values or deeply rooted experiences. Maybe you have personal experience similar to one of the cases. Perhaps you or someone you know benefitted or was hurt by being on one side or the other. In that case, you may have strong feelings about who is right and who is wrong.

Consider that your history, personal experience, and present concerns determine who you think is right.

What about the case of union and management at the manufacturing plant? Did you grow up in a union family? Are you a member of an organized bargaining unit? Do you remember the Air Traffic Controllers' strike of 1982? Whose side were you on? Did you see it as an issue of safety? Did you feel the controllers were overpaid prima donnas? If you witnessed that moment of history, you probably have some opinion about who is right, or at least a preference in the matter.

Perhaps the third scenario hits home. Do you love animals? Are you indifferent to them? What sort of teenage pranks did you pull?

Are you a white-collar manager? Have you been laid off or watched your fellows, members of your professional community, suffer at the hands of a corporate rightsizing or renewal? Have you seen your friends or family unable to find a job commensurate with their experience and skills?

The Endless Conflict of Right and Wrong

What is your opinion? You may say, *Well, the case studies do not reveal enough to discern who is right.* Or, *No one is right!* But did you notice that it is increasingly difficult to validate all parties in a squabble the closer the situation is to your personal experience? When a situation gets close enough it collapses into your strong and deeply held personal beliefs and becomes a matter of right and wrong, of personal principle.

Collapsing a viewpoint into right or wrong pits people against one another and brings human affairs to an impasse.

You are right and he is wrong. He thinks he is right and you are wrong. The remaining conversation becomes a verbal battle to prove and justify your opinion. The drive to overcome the other party is so strong it can lead to physical blows. Two high-tech vice presidents resort to slugging it out in the corporate parking lot in full view of their employees. What do you suppose brings them to such a state? It may seem funny to imagine two business executives in suit and tie busting each other's faces, but it was not intended for comic relief. What about the war in Bosnia? How many lives has it cost because people refuse to live as neighbors? Why have the Irish and the English wreaked unending destruction and violence upon one another for centuries? And much closer to home, what unresolved conflicts or standoffs are you engaged in at this time? When did you last have a perhaps polite but unyielding disagreement with someone on the job? What about a stubborn exchange with your husband or teenager? When have you dug your heels in and refused to budge? These are the arenas where you are right and you are convinced the other person is wrong.

The mindset of right and wrong is at the heart of every unresolved human conflict.

Wherever you are stuck in conflict, consider that what is at stake is not the specific issue but your insistence on dominating the other person with the rightness of your opinion or the wrongs of hers. Consider that right-wrong thinking is itself just a perspective, just one of many ways of looking at the world. Other philosophies and cultures are not so addicted to the assignment of right or wrong labels. Joseph Campbell points out that Eastern religions espouse a middle path. The middle path lies between good and evil, sees the validity and excess of each, and succumbs to the influence of neither.

Have you ever noticed that attempts to dictate right and wrong often backfire? For example, the last 30 years have witnessed attempts to legislate the goodness of racial equality through such programs as affirmative action. Today those programs are being attacked as a source of continuing bigotry and racial disharmony; critics say the programs perpetuate the very wrongs they were designed to right. When you operate from a perspective of right and wrong, whatever people or movements you place in the wrong will resist you. The more you push, the greater the resistance. Your only possible options are then to use overwhelming force to crush the resistors absolutely, or to live in a perpetual state of conflict.

When you push against something you consider wrong, it will push back against you. Uninterrupted, these actions set up a cycle of endless conflict.

The alternative is to grant a legitimacy to the opposing view, grant its right to exist even if you do not agree with it, and seek ways to find common ground. The chamber of commerce of a large midwestern city consists of corporate men and women with no experience dealing with unions. When they seek to intervene in a threatened teachers' strike, their first move is not to approach the teachers, but to attack them in the press. This, of course, creates a backlash which comes within days of causing a strike. Fortunately, the chamber ceases its public attacks, and extends an olive branch which quickly leads to cooperative projects and plans that benefit everyone.

> It may be that reaching out to others and including everyone is the best policy.

BE RIGHT OR BE SUCCESSFUL

It may seem to you that, *Right is RIGHT!* and not a matter of choice. If you take this stance, you will face unresolved conflicts that can erode your success and happiness throughout your life. Your rightness will hurt the relationships you have and will block you from forming other relationships.

> Assigning the labels of right and wrong will cost you love and success.

There is no successful and joyful marriage in which both parties have not given up the *right to be right* time and again. Any victory that makes the opposition permanently wrong breeds permanent hostility. Perhaps the greatest U.S. achievement in World War II was not the victory, but rather the policy toward former enemies after the war. The Marshall Plan and other efforts at rebuilding Europe and Japan created decades of prosperity for everyone, the United States included.

Today he is one of the union leaders at a processing plant. But in 1968, on his 18th birthday, the company calls him and tells him to report to work. When he shows up the foreman will only speak to him to give him orders; his co-workers will not speak to him at all. At lunch he sits alone and when he leaves at the end of the day, the tires on his car are slashed. These indignities do not deter this man and today he says simply, *Who would have thought then that the time would come when I would be an elected official for the union in this plant?* Asked if he holds grudges, this African-American says only,

---

If you hold grudges, after 27 years there would be a lot of people you would not speak to.

Insisting you are right is a good way to make enemies among co-workers and family.

Where in your life are you choosing to be right rather than to accomplish a goal?

What is the cost of the controversy over the lime-green house? What is ahead for the workers who depend on the manufacturing plant to support their families? Who wins when members of a community take emotionally charged sides over a dead cat? And for how long is the price paid?

GO BEYOND RIGHT AND WRONG

See the Other Perspective

Sometimes it is easy to see another person's perspective; sometimes it is not. The managers at the manufacturing plant can understand why the hourly employees are upset. As line workers, their jobs are in jeopardy from increasing automation. It is likely that many jobs will be lost in the next few years. More difficult for the managers to understand is why the employees are uncooperative and inflexible. As the managers see it, hostile behavior only increases the likelihood that the company will close the plant.

A worker with a stellar performance and attendance record arrives fifteen minutes late for his shift. He calls the manager from the guard gate and asks whether he will receive a mark against his attendance. The manager is sorry to tell him that, according to the contract, there is no choice but to give him a tardiness point and dock his pay for the time missed. The employee says then that he might as well go home, which he does. The manager is mystified. For want of 15 minutes, the mill employee sacrifices an entire day's wages. The only interpretation the manager can make is that the employee feels no obligation to his job or to the company. The manager analyzes the situation by comparing the worker's behavior to his own: *I would not have done that because I care about my job.*

Everything anyone ever does is absolutely consistent with the facts as they see, believe, and understand them to be.

The manager sees the worker's decision to leave from his own perspective on responsibility. Is there another way to view the situation? Why would someone with a near-perfect attendance record get out of bed, go through the trouble and effort to get dressed, eat breakfast, and show up at work simply to return home? This is not a matter of losing a quarter hour of pay. To the worker who leaves rather than passively accepting the blotch on his record, it may look more like he has been beaten by inflexible rules. When you are beaten, you might as well go home.

Why would employees anywhere resist change when it only means that the worst of their fears are more likely to come true? The line workers at the manufacturing plant are increasing the odds of losing their jobs when they express anger toward management. Yet, if you do not trust what management says, then when managers tell you that unless production improves you will lose your job, why would you believe the managers? You may suspect that no matter what you do the job is lost anyway and what remains is to collect your pay for the interim.

Your greatest leverage for accomplishing your goals, is to see the other person's perspective. It will be neither inferior nor illogical, and in its own context, it will be complete.

> Each personal perspective is legitimate and contains a complete and consistent view of the world as that person is able to see it.

A man who is thrown into anguish when he receives a single tardy mark on his record must have exceedingly high standards. Such a man has much to contribute and is worthy of respect. He is the antithesis of an irresponsible man and to confuse the two is to insult him and waste a great human resource.

Try a New Perspective

Here is an interesting exercise you can try for yourself. Find someone with no talent at catching a ball, perhaps a family member or office colleague. Ask the person to stand about 20 feet away and catch a tennis ball you will toss. Toss the ball, and watch the person fumble for it. Do this several times. Now change the instructions. Tell the person not to worry about whether they catch the ball or not. Instead, explain that the person is to concentrate on reporting to you which direction (up, down, left, or right) the seams are spinning as the ball comes toward him or her. Try this tactic several times.

What you will notice, if you look for it, is an amazing improvement in the person's ability and grace at catching the ball under the second set of instructions. If you are really ambitious, you can videotape the exercise to prove to yourself that the effect is real.

This simple exercise shows a profound phenomenon. Our actions result from our perspective. When you shift the perspective, you shift the actions.

Each person's actions are the naturally occurring result of what he or she perceives.

How does the world look to a hundred middle managers who attend numerous classes in leadership training and, yet, according to their executive bosses, do not change their management style? Consider the world for one of them. He is sitting at his desk, in his office, with his secretary outside the door answering the phone and, as she has always done, screening the callers according to her sense of who should be allowed to speak with him. He has just returned from a three-day class in leadership thinking that encourages him to be collaborative and allow the people who report to him greater autonomy to do their jobs effectively. This first morning back on the job he is planning a staff meeting to share his new-found ideas when his vice president calls demanding to know why the XYZ project is two months behind schedule. The time slippage must be recovered because there are customers waiting for the product. The vice president points out that if the manager is unable to get the project back on track then the project can be reassigned to someone else. So the manager calls the project leader into his office for an update. She tells him that the technicians are already working 60-hour weeks and it will be counterproductive to pressure them further. She suggests that upper management should not have made an unrealistic promise to the customer as there is no way to accelerate the delivery date. He wonders if there is someone else he can assign as project lead and decides that today is not the time to announce greater autonomy for everyone in the department. Perhaps next week will be better. And so it goes. The manager has not just made a choice to retain an obsolete management style. He has also chosen to remain in an environment where new actions appear to make no sense.

In every facet of your life you are continually choosing to do something and, equally, not to do something else. You make these selections to achieve a specific outcome, and believe that your choices are optimum to produce the intended result. Yet what if they are not?

> Actions are based on perspective. What if an alternate perspective would be more productive for what you want to achieve?

A recent news feature compares the success of several programs to enable people to break the cycle of drug addiction. The reporter observes that the programs with the highest rates of success are those that in some way acknowledge the existence of God or a supreme being. However, due to the separation of church and state, those programs are not eligible for government funding. From the news feature, it appears the mindset to keep the church out of government may not be optimal in substance-abuse recovery. This does not mean that one mindset is better than the other, but one may be more effective to achieve a stated goal.

Dom, top executive from a large heavy-equipment manufacturer, is laid off. No matter, he uses his large severance package to buy an Alpha Graphics franchise. He opens his new copy center business in a well-chosen location. Being a top executive, he sets up an expensive office in the back, hires a personal secretary, and never meets with customers nor personally staples their copy jobs. Those details are left to hired employees—just as they were in the days on executive row. The franchise fails.

Across town, Tina also buys an Alpha Graphics franchise, investing her life savings and going heavily into debt. Her location seems less promising than Dom's, but when customers walk into the store, Tina greets them by name and attentively listens to their needs. She gives them the impression that the job matters as much to her as it does to them. She personally checks every detail and always remembers to smile. Her franchise succeeds.

From what perspective is Dom viewing his franchise? Is it the most effective for his new circumstances? What other actions might have achieved better results?

All of us have our blind spots. Where in your professional or personal life are you not getting the results you intend? Perhaps you are tackling the problem from a limited or even misleading perspective.

During the Vietnam war, a soldier with his platoon is engaged in a battle with the Vietcong at the edge of the jungle. Both sides are hunkered down and shoot at one another for two days. A primitive stone wall stretches across the battlefield as the demarcation between them. Toward dusk on the second day there is the sound of chanting and, from one end, a Buddhist monk climbs on the wall and begins walking directly into the line of fire. He is followed a few feet behind by another monk, then a third and so on. The firing stops. Silence falls over the soldiers as they watch with awe the unhurried movement of the contingent of monks. When they reach the opposite end of the wall, the monks climb down and one by one disappear into the forest. But the fighting is now over; no one has the stomach for more killing. The night is peaceful and in the morning both groups break camp and move on. What happened? What is the perspective of the monks? How does the world look to them that they climb upon a wall in full view of warring soldiers and walk calmly and safely through their midst?

> Perhaps another perspective would be more helpful in achieving your objectives.

Whatever you would like to accomplish—a great workplace for your employees, a good marriage, a productive relationship with your co-workers—there is some way of looking at the situation, perhaps at present unknown to you, that will allow you to achieve these goals. What might it be? How can you find it?

Master Change

What is your experience with change? The commonly accepted thinking is that people resist change. Business courses teach strategies for change and caution that changes cannot be made overnight. Yet this is not our experience, and it is probably not yours either. The only way that changes are ever made is overnight. You may spend time preparing for change but as for the change itself, you just do it. Furthermore, you have probably experienced many changes that you were excited and thrilled about making and for which you could hardly wait. Getting your driver's license when you turned 16 may have been such a heady experience. Perhaps you remember graduating from school, starting a full-time job and making your entry into adult society? Or what about the birth of your first child? Did you look forward to the event with joy and anticipation? With none of these momentous changes did you know what to expect, and yet you rushed forward to meet them brimming with energy. What was so different about these events as compared to the changes that you resist?

Common wisdom holds that the hardest thing to change is people. We disagree. It may be hard to move heavy equipment, to change the course of a river by dredging, or to move all of your furniture and repaint your living room. But to change your mind, to change your perspective, is easy and involves no heavy lifting.

The perspective of right and wrong admits of no change. To master change, abandon the perspective of right and wrong.

A manager at a large manufacturing plant is responsible for implementing major automation changes. He knows that the key to success is to have the employees buy into his project. So he sets out to sell them on the idea without, at first, a great deal of success. The employees push back. When he realizes the employees are operating from a negative mindset toward change he adopts a completely new and risky approach. He meets with the affected employees and explains what is happening in the industry, the equipment available, and the consequences of automating or not. He asks them what should be done—to automate or not—and tells them he will abide by their decision. He knows it could threaten his career to go back to corporate and turn down the capital funds. But he also knows the automation will be a poor investment unless the employees back the changes. The employees know they hold the future of the plant in their hands. They vote unanimously for automation and 80 percent of them ask to participate in the changeover.

Gain Perspective on Perspectives

There are many perspectives available for every situation you face. Some work better than others. Yet most of us do not readily discard outmoded or inappropriate perspectives even when we can see they are not working. Why not? What prevents us from changing to a suitable or workable view of the world to achieve our goals?

A major credit card company is losing the battle for plastic spending to competitors. Marketing devises a strategy to provide a grace period for charges due, that is, to delay interest charges for customer purchases. They call it *Interest Free* and launch a major marketing campaign. To modify the computer systems to delay the interest charges is a harrowing task, and the team of technicians responsible to do this is understaffed, overburdened, and exhausted. This group, however, has recently been given autonomy from traditional management direction and is now a pilot self-managed team. In a radical departure from the usual work situation, the team can set its own schedules, determine its own delivery dates, and obtain needed resources on its own authority. This crucial project is a test for both the team and the self-managed-team concept. To succeed the team must deliver, thus proving that self-direction gets the job done on schedule, without a manager overseeing the progress. Throughout the project, the team operates with increasing effectiveness and high morale among the participants. In the end, they meet their promised delivery dates against tremendous odds.

In spite of their remarkable success, the self-managed team is disbanded and replaced with the traditional management structure. The *Interest Free* team has shown that extraordinary results are possible without management. Why, then, is it disbanded? The answer is that the entire structure of the company assumes multiple layers of management with attendant pay scales, performance assessments, and all manner of power and authority. An alternative system, even when it is more productive, is unworkable as well as unacceptable. The company is more committed to management hierarchy than to productivity and profits.

> Most of us are more interested in our perspective being right than in the rightness of our perspective.

Can business be successful without heavy-handed management? Dave Marsing manages Intel Corporation's Fab 11, one of the most sophisticated, high-pressure, high-stakes factories in the world. Yet he is a gentle man who studies Zen and ends each meeting with a soft-spoken *OK, now what can I do for you?* He believes, *Having to change your life when you arrive at work each morning is tantamount to slavery.* His view of his role is to help and serve, teach and mentor, not to direct. This perspective works well. It has to. Fab 11 is Intel's largest factory.[1] Marsing did not always work this way, not until his

---

[1]"Killer Results without Killing Yourself," by Michael S. Malone, *Fast Company*, Volume 1, Number 1, 1995, p.124ff.

heart attack. After that, he found the motivation to learn new techniques for managing. Is it possible to learn from Dave Marsing's example that there are exciting perspectives in management that warrant exploration?

Your perspective—your particular view of reality—drives your every action, inaction, and reaction. Change your perspective and your behavior will change spontaneously and with ease. Enable others to alter their perspective and you will have created a powerful community of friends. The next chapter addresses the means to surface old perspectives and create new ones to enable you to alter your behavior to reflect your intentions and achieve your goals.

> Your perspective is not right or wrong. It is merely your perspective.

ACHIEVE YOUR GOALS

At the beginning of the chapter, we asked you to make note of some personal or professional objectives, some areas where you would like to make better progress. Now, using the ideas in this chapter, reconsider your issues in light of these questions.

- ♦ *From what perspective are you viewing your area of dissatisfaction? Can you write down characteristics of that perspective? Pretending that you are someone else, rewrite your problem statement in six different ways. Write about it as seen from: 1) a tragic perspective, 2) a problem-solving perspective, 3) a humorous perspective, 4) a grateful perspective, 5) an enemy's perspective, and 6) a child's perspective.*
- ♦ *For any conflict you are involved in, make a list of the issues and assumptions that you are certain you are right about. Would the other party in the dispute agree that these assumptions are right?*

♦ *With regard to people who are resisting you, make a list of all the things—assumptions, behaviors, and beliefs—that they are wrong about. Make a list of all the ways in which you have communicated to them that they are wrong. Are you willing to allow them to have their perspective and not judge them as wrong?*

5

Fulfill Your Future

We must dare to think *unthinkable thoughts*. We must learn to confront all the options and possibilities that confront us in a complex and rapidly changing world. We must learn to welcome and not to fear the voices of dissent. We must dare to think about *unthinkable things* because when things become unthinkable, thinking stops and action becomes mindless.

... SENATOR WILLIAM FULBRIGHT, SENATE SPEECH, MARCH 27, 1964

21ST-CENTURY THINKING

The 21st century will be one of intense relativism. Beyond change in technology, institutions, and borders we will see radical and unceasing change in truth itself.

No single truth that has ever given stability and order to the human world will go unchallenged.

There will be no center, no bedrock of belief, no philosophy, no guiding political, social, or organizational principle for anyone to rely on or use as a foundation for living for any length of time. Change has become meta-change—continuous transformation in what human beings believe about themselves.

But this is not bad news. While a suspension of life's rules may seem threatening at first, it is also key to genuine freedom, new results, and unlimited possibility. Americans especially should understand this, as the unlimited frontier was in fact, and still is in legend, the defining characteristic of American culture. But now, instead of unlimited land, the opportunity lies in unlimited thinking as the rules of the 20th-century workplace fall away.

We live under a vast, unquestioned, cultural assumption, despite massive evidence to the contrary, that our circumstances are real. Nothing could be further from the truth. There is nothing whatsoever real about circumstances.

You and I create our circumstances through our interpretation of events.

And then we surrender that power of creation by assuming, in a way lost to consciousness, that those same circumstances were created by someone or something outside of us and beyond our control. That is, you and I place the power of reality in whatever is going on around us, rather than realizing that we and only we create reality.

There is a way of thinking, little known or used in recent times, ideal for handling meta-change. To use it, you do not act on the situation directly, but rather, you alter the conceptual rules that hold the situation in place.

Perspectives and Realities

At the world's largest flour mill, automation has resulted in continuous worker attrition for the past 20 years. The dwindling band of remaining workers is depressed and despondent. They grieve for their lost colleagues and wish they would return, somehow. They see little future for themselves.

However, the workers who have been let go have, after a period of adjustment, done quite well. One works in car sales, another in a network marketing arrangement, and a third owns several cabs. They are not sad, but rather are getting on with their lives. The sad ones are the workers left in the dwindling mill. Clearly, those who have left and those left behind live in different realities and have different interpretations about the same "objective" situation, namely the fact of automation-driven layoffs at the flour mill.

The flour mill, and possibly your own situation, shows how perspectives work. Your particular perspective, your view, becomes the only possible view, in terms of determining your feelings and actions. The people at the flour mill assume that the flour mill is their only possible world. This blinds them to the accomplishments of the departees and blinds them to similar possibilities for themselves. The perspective of limited possibility also makes them less effective than they might be in their current jobs.

Sometimes we shift our interpretation, which allows us to enter another world of opportunities. Usually it takes an external event, a catastrophe of some sort, such as being laid off. But why must this be so? Why cannot the remaining employees at the flour mill realize that they could choose among an incredible array of lifestyles, careers, jobs, and ways of making it in the world? Instead, their reality is the flour mill, with its dwindling labor pool. They are stuck because they feel stuck.

Alternate Realities

If you review the history of your company and study different divisions within it (such as marketing, engineering, manufacturing, and finance), you will see overwhelming evidence that different people see reality in radically different ways. For example, in introducing a new cereal, manufacturing worries about the practicalities of production. Cereal, which most of us take for granted, involves enormous and complex machinery husbanded by skilled operators and engineers. By contrast, marketing worries about sensory appeal—taste, crunch, color, solubility in milk, and even non-nutritious ways for children to use cereal. Marketing designed one cereal as footballs so that kids could flick cereal pieces through goal posts.

Thus marketing and manufacturing view the same reality—cereal—from entirely different vantage points. The problem arises in that the separate camps have little appreciation for the other's view. As another example, the public school system of a major midwestern city suffers from contentious and divisive relationships among the unions, the school administration, and the business community. There are frequent, acrimonious articles in the local paper and a constant personal undermining of one another both in public and private. When you speak with individuals from any of the constituent groups, they present the most convincing case as to why they are in the right and the other groups are either incompetent or sinister. The teachers' union, for instance, says that the administration is out to strip their contract. For their part, the administration says that the teachers' primary interest is in emasculating the administration and making them look like fools to the public.

Personal Perspectives

Your personal perspective determines, not just how you will react and behave, but also what you are able to perceive, what you value and pay attention to, indeed your total reality as you construe it. For example, if you always look at your house only from ground level, you cannot see the roof. If the shingles are deteriorating, you will not see this from your vantage point on the ground, nor will you undertake repairs. To do anything about conditions on the roof, you must first go up there and look at it. If your system of home maintenance relies solely on information you gather from the ground view, your perspective is deficient and inadequate. You may not realize the danger today, but you will have trouble eventually. The gutters will come loose, and the shingles will blow away. If you never walk on the roof, the consequences of your limited perspective may someday damage the interior of your house.

All personal perspectives are limited and insufficient in the view they provide of our environment.

We think we have the roof of our reality nailed. Then one day we learn that our skills are obsolete, our spouse has walked out, or we are about to lose our job, and we have no idea how these catastrophes have come to happen.

The limitations of personal perspective affect the Queen of England and the president of IBM every bit as much as they affect the rest of us.

Furthermore, different individuals have different perspectives, different views of the world. Without tolerance and openness to these, we are likely to devalue others who construe reality differently. A classic example is the relationship between marketing and manufacturing or engineering in many companies. At one company, the marketing people call the engineers *dweebs* whereas the engineers speak of the marketing folks as *useless parasites with technical pretensions*. Needless to say, these groups do not work well together.

Many personal perspectives are organized around core values or themes. A building is filled with software engineers. Theirs is a perspective that values precision, rigor, and engineering excellence. In this community, one of the most valued skills is the ability to find flaws, holes in reasoning and architecture, bugs in the code. Prestige accrues to the most critical, aloof, and penetrating engineers. One day, a marketing film is scheduled to be shot in the building. Professional actors, flamboyantly dressed, arrive in a limousine. They breeze through the halls, laughing and impersonating famous personalities. The contrast of perspectives is striking. Is the bastion of serious engineering a temple of commitment to quality or is it a staid and sexless place where people waste their lives glued to glass tubes? Are the actors a breath of life, with access to passion and adventure, or are they flakes?

One enormous possibility of 21st-century thinking is openness to and active exploration of other perspectives, other realities. Open communication is the essential tool.

> Each of us has the choice—whether to trash and find fault in other people's perspectives or to sample, explore, and find value.

The ability to see beyond your own and others' current perspectives and to shift and play with other realities is absolutely crucial to survival and prosperity in the 21st-century work world. What are some steps you can take to master this art? The first is to explore your own mind and see how it determines reality as you know it.

> It is an incredible advantage to be the master of one's perspective rather than simply falling into it by virtue of current circumstances.

You can recognize people who have this power. They seem always to be driving their own destiny, creating their own reality. Successful entrepreneurs always have this quality because the heart of entrepreneurship is creating new realities in the domain of business.

21ST-CENTURY PERSPECTIVES

A new kind of perspective is needed for 21st-century thinking—a future-focused perspective, spontaneous and flexible, and applicable to many different life situations. Twenty-first century thinking builds on the idea of context. Context is the set of circumstances that surround an event. Twenty-first-century thinking holds that surrounding circumstances not only give meaning to the event, they are *integral* to its occurrence.

Twenty-first-century perspective asserts that surrounding
circumstances are inseparable from the event.

As you can see, this differs from more traditional ways of thinking
such as scientific, mechanistic, systems-oriented, or bureaucratic. The
differences are fundamental. Twenty-first-century thinking defines differently such seemingly basic and obvious concepts as perception, reality, facts, evidence, and cause and effect.

What Are the Facts?

In 21st-century thinking, there are no such things as neutral facts.

Every so-called fact springs from and contains within it
assumptions, prejudices, and a hidden agenda.

A chamber of commerce in a large midwestern city learns this to
their sorrow. Anxious to improve the public school system and heal
poor relationships among the community, the school administration,
and the teachers' union, the chamber funds a supposedly objective report to study the existing school district labor contracts. The result is a
fire storm of acrimony and bad feelings. For one thing, the auditors
commissioned to produce the report have, unknown to the chamber, a
history of participating in anti-union efforts. The *facts* of the matter are
so complex and numerous that any effort to say anything at all about
them, even to select which facts to analyze, can be made only from
some perspective. For example, the auditors choose to report on a contract provision that specifies that teachers' break rooms must be sup-
plied with coffee machines equipped with automatic shutoffs. How
absurd, how trivial, implies the report. But ignored in the report are the

many nationally acclaimed and innovative educational initiatives the teachers have created and implemented over the past decades.

In other words, why did the auditors choose to focus on coffee machine clauses and not innovative educational accomplishments? It is because, like all of us, they can perceive and report only on that slice of reality permitted by their personal perspective.

This inability to look outside our own perspective has consequences in our ability to succeed in any business endeavor. Consider the simple, standard paper clip known as the GEM design. This 100-year-old design dominates the paper clip industry—you have dozens of them in your desk. The design consists of a piece of wire bent double in three places. Over the years hundreds of patents have been granted for alternative designs, virtually every one of which does a better job than the GEM design of holding papers together. But none has been a significant commercial success. Why? Because the inventors ignored the context of paper clip use—most paper clips are not used to hold papers at all. Rather they are used to fiddle with or unbent to create interesting sculptures or to extract dirt from beneath fingernails. Plastic clips, flat clips, clips with little circular bends in them—none come close to the GEM design as a fiddling, artistic design, or dirt-removal tool.

Twenty-first century thinking calls us to focus, not on facts, but on the context that gives facts their meaning. This view is one of the fundamental perspective shifts that will benefit you in 21st-century work.

What Proof Do You Have?

Another crucial shift in 21st-century thinking is to focus, not on past evidence, but on future possibilities. Indeed, the concept of evidence itself has no meaning in contextual thinking because, contextually, every situation is unique and therefore outcomes cannot be predicted based on past experience.

As a practical example of the difference this way of thinking makes to business practice, consider the problem of finding suitable employees for a job. According to traditional thinking, you would look into the person's past history and experience for evidence that they could perform well. In a stable world, where the job yesterday is much the same as today, this makes sense.

> In the 21st century of meta-change, looking at past history
> may not just be irrelevant, it may even be counterproductive.
> According to contextual thinking, therefore, you would not
> use past history as a criterion for selection!

This may not sound so strange when you look at examples of uneasiness with the traditional practice of filling positions on the basis of experience. In national politics there is a perennial movement to impose term limits on political officeholders. Thus, some percentage of the population considers prior job experience to be a detriment for presidents, senators, and representatives.

Two consultants are effective in helping a large industrial plant improve labor relations, reduce grievances, and boost productivity. They come to the situation fresh and use methods unheard of in that union environment. When the project is successful, the union vice president pays them an interesting compliment: *Anyone who knew what they were doing couldn't have done what you did.* Contextually, this makes great sense. With a fresh perspective and unfettered by history and tradition, the consultants can see solutions and courses of action that are invisible to others more steeped in the environment. In general, any consultant knows that a great deal of his or her value depends on a fresh perspective toward the situation. If the consultant gets too experienced, too indoctrinated by the client's culture, the consultant's value is lost.

To take another example of uneasiness with past experience, the mid-1990s continue to be a time of massive corporate layoffs. AT&T announces the layoff of 40,000 middle managers in early 1996. The individuals made redundant are, for the most part, people with long service and vast experience in running a telecommunications system. Apparently though, whoever decided on the layoffs concluded that these people are not capable of making money through their efforts within the new context of AT&T as its leaders define it. Their experience in what was once a bastion of monopolistic bureaucracy is now a detriment.

Twenty-first-century thinking focuses on future possibilities, not past evidence. Evidence ties us to the past. Possibility alters the future.

What Caused This?

One holdover from 20th-century mechanistic thinking is a belief that analyzing situations in terms of cause and effect is useful. We think that to get a desired result, we need to take deliberate and focused action—that there is a one-to-one predictable relationship between what happens first and what happens next. This reasoning is practical for many physical phenomena, but not for human affairs.

> With regard to human affairs, there are deep problems with cause and effect thinking.

There are always an infinite number of things happening in the human world, and the world itself is constantly changing. Nothing holds still long enough to adequately determine which actions will produce desired results. There is always something else going on in the wings to disrupt the plans. For example, in a company of any size, there is no way to satisfactorily analyze the contribution each employee makes to the bottom line. A hot sales representative lands a $10 million contract with the government for computer-switching equipment. Did she cause the $10 million sale? If not all of it, then how much? Obviously she contributed, but there could have been no contract if there were no switching equipment to begin with. The switching equipment was designed by engineering and built by manufacturing. Did they cause the sale? But if there were no founders, there would be no company at all, and hence no engineering and manufacturing departments. Were the founders the cause? Well, there would have been no founders without investors, so maybe the investors are the real cause. But wait, there would have been no investors without mothers, so could it be that the investors' mothers are the real cause?

As you can see, any real situation is so complex, with so many possible chains and analyses, that the notion of cause and effect as a useful analytical tool collapses. Therefore, the 21st-century perspective is to abandon the notion of cause and effect in matters relating to people and to assume instead that actions and results emerge spontaneously from the appropriate context.

> The 21st-century thinker focuses primarily on creating the right context and focuses on action only secondarily.

Consider the specific case of doctors, nurses, aides, housekeeping and administration in a hospital. Who is it that causes the patient to get well? The traditional answer to this question is the doctors, so they are highly paid and held in awe. But anyone who has stayed in a hospital knows that nurses who are upbeat and reassuring create an entirely different environment from nurses who are harried and sloppy. Lackadaisical housekeeping also has a depressing impact. In short, everyone in the hospital contributes to surroundings that either promote healing and wellness or do not. Twenty-first-century thinking postulates that it is the entire context-for-wellness rather than any single cause that affects the patients. From this you can see why teams can be almost inexplicably powerful to achieve business goals. In the effort to attain high-performance teamwork, 21st-century organizations focus on empowering everyone to take responsibility for the outcome, not just a few so-called key people. As a result a context develops within the team which spontaneously produces the desired results.

What Really Happened?

Perhaps the biggest obstacle to happy and fulfilling 21st-century work is our Western cultural habit, addiction really, to negativism and criticism. The negative kills the positive. To see this, try suggesting a radical and far-out idea at your next meeting. Make note of the reactions. You are almost certain to find that the overwhelming majority of the reactions are criticisms, cautions, warnings, and reasons-why-not. Or pick up any newspaper and analyze a few articles for the percentage of sentences that generate possibility and express enthusiasm for new ideas as opposed to the number of sentences that tear down, criticize, and explain why some new initiative cannot possibly work.

Under the operating assumption that the world is fixed and real, independent of our observations about it, negative statements can be justified as objectively reporting facts.

Under the operating assumption that the human world is created by our characterization of it, however, negative reporting actually creates a negative world.

Similarly, positive reporting creates a positive world.

Suppose you attend a department-wide meeting, the purpose of which is to talk about future direction and objectives. As you leave the meeting, you encounter a recently hired colleague. He was detained, missed the meeting, and now asks you what happened. You respond cynically, *Just more of the same old nonsense about how we all need to work our fingers to the bone. The boss must need a new vacation home so we have to earn him a bigger bonus. You're lucky you didn't have to sit through it!* Can you see the reality that is created by your words? You may think you are describing the lay of the land but, actually, you are creating the backdrop against which you and your fellow employee will work. Suppose instead you choose to say, *It was a really valuable meeting and it's a shame you missed it. The boss gave us an overview of what's happening throughout the company. It's clear our work in this department is crucial to the company's success!* Can you see the entirely different reality that you have just created for your co-worker? Now consider the aggregate of all the remarks that you make about the meeting. Do not forget those you make that are repeated by others. Whatever you say, others will jump on the bandwagon and make the same pronouncement.

The outcome of what you say passes for objective reality, but there is nothing objective about it. It is your creation.

ENTER THE 21ST CENTURY

How will you be successful in the 21st century? What will matter *will not* be skills, credentials, or brilliant proposals. What *will* matter is your ability to *fit in* with other people. This is *fitting in* to their world and perspectives. When you are accepted by others and are yourself at ease with them, what you accomplish and what is accomplished by the people around you becomes extraordinary.

Your ability to appreciate, enter, and affect the different perspectives of the people you meet is the essential skill of the 21st-century workplace.

This section outlines seven behaviors that you will find especially valuable to enter into others' perspectives. When you do this, you naturally and easily form productive and satisfying relationships for the 21st-century workplace.

Enjoy and Appreciate Other Perspectives

The first behavior is simply to learn enjoyment in what is different from you. If you are a tourist, the point of your journey is to appreciate and admire the people and customs you encounter. The idea of visiting the Cajun bayou region is to experience and enjoy, among other things, their exciting music, spicy food, and unique philosophy of life. This attitude will serve you well to explore the perspectives of other people. So, for example, when you meet union members recall that they belong to a proud tradition that has won, through blood and sacrifice, dignity and decency for workers who were once treated as slaves. When you visit England, remember that it ruled the greatest empire the world has ever known. That accomplishment, by people of a small and isolated island, deserves respect. When you meet middle managers, remind yourself that they are the glue that holds organizations together and their job is impossible. Your country neighbor, whose house peels paint, has adopted two children with disabilities. Will you focus on the peeling paint or the generosity of giving unwanted kids a life? Can you admit, however reluctantly, that the vice president who rejected your proposal is a master at shaking things up and setting new directions for the organization?

> When you meet people, listen for what is valuable in their unique perspective.

The founder and president of Sony, Akihito Morita, has selected a successor with no technical background and one who was not formerly employed at Sony. The new president is an artist and aspiring symphony conductor. Morita-san wants an artist and outsider, not a technician, to run his company in the 21st century.

Adopt and Adapt to Other Perspectives

As you explore different worlds in the course of your 21st-century career, you will find that people have perceptions, values, and beliefs unimaginably different from your own.

Do you know, for example, that many cultures of the world place relationships before being on time? Thus, if you have a meeting in Paris or Mexico City, your counterparts may be late, not because they disrespect you, but because they live according to the needs of the people they are with at the moment and not by your calendar. Of course, once they meet with you, you receive the same priority. If you insist on punctuality and let everyone know your poor opinion of people who are late, it will not form a strong basis for working with them.

Wayne has the task of forging a strategic relationship between his fledgling U.S. high-technology startup firm and a large Japanese organization. There is a problem, though. Wayne used to work for another U.S. technology company and while there negotiated deals with the same Japanese company he now seeks a new alliance with. Shortly after Wayne left, the first company proved unable to fulfill the agreements with its Japanese partner. In Western culture, this does not matter. Have you noticed that when someone leaves a job, their commitments and responsi-bilities disappear overnight? Jim promises to get back to you, he doesn't, and three weeks later you call to find out why. *Oh, James is no longer with us,* you hear. And that settles the matter. In Japan, however, your commitments are considered to come from you, not your position or even your company. If you make a promise you are expected to see that it is honored, and if it is not, you are disgraced. *Leaving the company* is not an excuse.

In his new position, Wayne travels to Japan and is granted a meet-ing with top executives. It will be his last, unless he is able to speak effec-tively into their listening. His action is almost unheard of among Western executives. He humbles himself and makes profound and sincere apolo-gies for the disruptions he caused by leaving his former employer and not ensuring that his promises to the firm were met. He takes full responsi-bility and vows that he will respect the sanctity of the business relation-ship. The Japanese executives are impressed with such behavior from a Western businessman, and choose his new company, not just to be a busi-ness partner, but to join their keiretsu (business family), a multinational conglomerate with almost one trillion (yes, trillion) dollars in annual sales. This act ensures a bright future for Wayne's new company.

In the 21st century adopting the customs of another gives honor and earns respect.

Invite Dynamic Exchange

The most interesting and valuable results happen when worlds interact with each other. The huge success of personal computers, for example, depends on perfectionist engineering combined with futuristic, vision-oriented daydreaming. Every business needs a critical, analytical focus on the numbers and also products and services that people want in the first place; somewhere along the line someone has to invent those prod-ucts and services.

One of the most expensive places to live is Palo Alto, California, in the heart of Silicon Valley. Is this because the climate is so pleasant? While the climate is pleasant, that is not the reason for property values of $1,000,000 for a quarter-acre lot. Property values are astronomical because the town is a thriving, networked community of inventors, investors, scientists, artists, and fast-thinking businesspeople, all of whom talk to each other. The fuel that fires the community is not the companies—those come and go at a bewildering pace—but rather the extensive interpersonal networking and openness to new ideas.

We all know how to open ourselves to new ideas. For example, the latest fashion in interior and exterior decoration is called feng-shui, the ancient Chinese art of decorating for harmonious living. This art carefully considers the proper use of color and the most efficacious alignment of furniture between the north–south poles. Decorators versed in this art are in great demand and able to charge hefty fees. Feng-shui shares a characteristic common to both kosher pickles and shamrocks. Each is an expression of a culture to which most of us do not belong. Yet, ever willing to adopt what is to our advantage, we eat kosher pickles and gladly celebrate St. Patrick's Day, wearing shamrocks and buttons that say *Kiss me, I'm Irish*.

> To carry this receptivity into other areas, we must trust that there are rewards and riches, as yet unknown, that will open to us when we do so.

We can learn a great deal from others not like ourselves, as in this encounter between a high-powered corporate businesswoman and a public health nurse. They meet at a class in teamwork. The public health nurse works with people who are disabled and elderly in an impoverished rural district. At first the businesswoman dismisses the nurse as kind but unsophisticated. During the class, however, the nurse jokes about her outrageous phone bills from calling state legislators and influential citizens to get support for special projects in the rural community. *Sometimes, she says thoughtfully, it is the only way I can get the job done.* The business manager is thunderstruck by the nurse's finesse. She realizes that she herself must pull out the stops to get the funding she needs for a crucial project. Immediately she asks the nurse to be her mentor. Once back on the job, she displays tenacity with her own senior management and wins their approval and the budget for her project.

Our best preparation for the 21st century will come from people who think differently than we do.

Whatever background you have, your experiences and perspectives are of immense value to many people and in many jobs. Take the time to explore strange, out-of-the-way ideas, people, and connections, for what you can give as well as receive.

Break Out

We are not our jobs or positions or titles. It is a serious and self-created problem if we imprison ourselves in whatever fixed category our employer places us. Each of us has a myriad of skills and is capable to succeed at many kinds of work. Even if you are immersed in your job today, it does not follow that it must always be so. The day may come when a particular view of yourself is *used up*. Perhaps you have achieved all there is for you in that job, and now you are uninspired, ready to move on.

For example, two women are among the upper managers for an international financial corporation. A significant restructuring eliminates 80 percent of the management positions in their division. Nonetheless, both are among the elite few who are offered the chance to keep their jobs. Both women refuse and seize this opportunity to redefine their careers. One is an expert in antique furniture and jewelry. She lives in the southwest near several retirement communities and sets up her own estate-disposition firm to handle the sale or auction of property for out-of-state heirs. The other takes advantage of the proximity and burgeoning trade with Central and South America to open an import-export business. Neither of these women define themselves as their corporate jobs or titles, much less their corporate skills. As a result, they are delighted with the opportunity to embark on new careers.

David, a graphic artist not in management, is laid off during a company crisis. He has been quite happy to work anonymously in a large company, but now through no desire of his own, he is on the street. His first choice is to go back to school and finish his degree in fine arts. To support himself, he sets up a business designing corporate-image packages for start-up entrepreneurs. Located in an area deluged with layoffs, his business flourishes. Two years later, with his degree in hand, he contemplates what he wants to do next. In the end, he follows his dreams and moves to Australia where he now owns and operates a graphic arts company.

In the 21st century you are whatever you choose to be.

Act in the Moment

Twenty-first-century contextual thinking reverses the traditional relationship between evidence and action. Traditionally, as part of our mechanistic heritage, we plan and analyze a situation and only when we have some comfort and certainty do we take action—*ready, aim, fire*. We do this to assure that the past, from which our evidence is derived, will be replayed and give us control over the outcome this time around.

This approach may yield the desired effect in an unchanging world, but can be irrelevant or counterproductive in a continuously transforming world. For example, a small company decides to buy a heavy-duty fax machine. The company forms a committee of all the department heads. The committee gets bids from vendors, analyzes and revises its equipment budget, surveys the user needs, and makes a seemingly careful decision. In the three months it takes the committee to do this, six new machines come on the market, the most expensive of which has more functions than, and costs half the price of, the least expensive model they were considering. But the planning process must be served, so the company buys the older, costlier model their planning has determined is best.

As you can see, the purchasing process ignores completely the role of the shifting context. That is, fax machines are being rapidly improved and the prices are dropping. Evidence about which model is the best buy is invalid when it does not consider those background events.

> If you place action before certainty in your endeavors, you will move fast, learn quickly, and grow rapidly.

Cathy is the knowledgeable owner of a successful women's clothing boutique. When she bought the business she knew nothing about retail sales. Browsing in a small dress shop, she mentions to the sales woman that she is possibly looking for a business to buy. The attendant, who is also the owner, immediately advises her that the boutique is up for sale. The idea captures Cathy's imagination and two weeks later, she owns the boutique. After the closing, at five o'clock on a winter evening, Cathy returns by herself to the store. *I spent the whole night figuring out how to tag the clothes. I just made up the prices. I was there until I opened the shop in the morning and through that first day. I never learned anything so fast in my life.* If Cathy had insisted that she must learn more about retail or if she waited for sufficient evidence that she could succeed, she would never have made what proved to be an extraordinarily successful purchase. The 21st century will provide each of us with opportunities for great risk and great reward. Only you can choose for yourself when and whether to act in the moment.

Invent Your Value

The world's most demanding skills have vanished, in terms of value. Consider, for example, the skills of pyramid design, colonial administration, sword forging, preserving meat in brine, wooden boat-building, and typesetting using hot metal. Generations were spent creating and mastering these skills, and in their time they tamed the world. Once skills took 100 years or more to run the course of their contribution. Today, the half-life of a specific skill is closer to 100 days.

> A skill is the ability to create value within a specific context.
> When the context disappears, so does the value of the skill.

Books and articles on how to cope with the future often stress the importance of skills. But skills have no absolute or permanent importance. No one really knows what skills are or how to measure them. The world of productive work changes so rapidly that specific skills rapidly become outdated, and it is next to impossible to predict what skills will be needed in the future. Skills are double-edged, just like language itself. Tom and Mark are skilled ex-IBM mainframe product managers. But they dare not put this information on their resumes. The job market actually considers these skills as a handicap, appropriate only in slow-moving, heavily bureaucratic organizations!

The one skill that will be extremely helpful is the skill to create value for your special abilities: the skill to invent skills. Leverage in the 21st century comes from defining your personal and unique kind of work. You will be the only person doing it, so you will get to make the rules.

> A skill worth having is the skill of inventing skills.

Gineen, an office manager, is laid off when the owner of her beauty salon suddenly dies. In desperation she accepts a part-time position as night manager for a retirement and nursing facility. She comes to love the residents, and they feel the same about her. Soon she is the recreation director. But the owners quickly realize she is also their best, though unofficial, sales person because of her engaging manner and sincere enthusiasm. When she refuses a sales position, they tell her to define her own job and set her own salary. The result is a well-paid, unique position that utilizes Gineen's personal and special talents.

Another woman, laid off with 60,000 others from a mega-corporation, undertakes to start a newsletter for the company's alumni. The newsletter is a rapid success and fills a deep void in the lives of the corporate expatriates. They can read about and learn from each other's successes and failures, keep valuable connections alive, find partners for new ventures, and advertise their new services to one another. The woman who invents the newsletter now makes over $100,000 a year from subscriptions and advertising.

Your best 21st-century job will be the one you invent.

Find Others Who Want to Find You

Someone will hire you or pay you money, if they see benefit to themselves greater than the cost of paying you. The catch is that they must see value within the world as they understand it. There are not less economic opportunities today, or even fewer jobs. Rather, there are more. There is no less work, just fewer steady jobs. Companies that downsize often follow this, sooner or later, with hiring back different people, or even hiring back as consultants and temporary personnel many of the same people they recently let go. Companies that permanently lose their stature often belong to industries that are expanding, only with different players. In its heyday, AT&T employed almost a million people. Today, it employs 300,000 and dropping. But the telecommunications industry as a whole—Sprint, MCI and numerous other carriers—still employs almost a million people. Additionally, the diversification of the industry has created more jobs in other industries, such as advertising, telemarketing, and credit services.

> In a slow-moving economy, power relies on sheer size. In a changing economy, power depends on flexibility.

The free marketplace provides an arena where flexibility and size are naturally reconciled. You can use this insight to personal advantage by choosing to operate in a context where, through flexibility, you connect with the people who will pay for your services. To do this you must find and connect genuinely with these people.

There are many ways to reach people, some as simple as an entrepreneurial window washer going from door to door. There are high-tech means as well. You can buy, for 20 dollars, a CD-ROM containing the names and addresses of every publicly registered company in the country, regardless of size. You can access, cheaply, enormous databases showing every article published in the national or regional press that mentions any of these companies. With tools such as these, you can explore virtually the entire world of work and craft innovative and personal communications to exactly the person who would be thrilled to work with you.

One fledgling public relations specialist uses high-tech, low-tech, and an old-fashioned request for help to reach her target market. First, she uses her CD-ROM to find a local union hall and calls to ask what publications are most widely read among the membership. The response directs her to the Manchester Union Leader. Using her Bacon's Media Directory, she learns the name of the editor and his phone number. Immediately she faxes off her first-ever press release. The next morning she calls the editor and asks, quite sincerely, if he will critique the press release she sent the day before. *Good thing you called*, he says, *or this would have been lost under a pile of paper*. He reads her write-up and tells her how to improve it. *Now see here*, he informs her, *we're too busy to do anything with this today but next week I'll send a reporter out to get an interview and we'll do a full write-up and photo.*

Information technology can get you quickly to the right person. But only genuine human connection will get you results.

Information technology has eliminated many routine jobs, but has also opened new possibilities for profitable human collaboration. The authors wrote this book, for example, simultaneously in New Hampshire and Arizona. They can transmit the draft of a chapter to one another in 30 seconds and the entire manuscript in 10 minutes, using normal phone lines and affordable computers. It is possible to work together intensively, and no one has to move.

THE POSSIBILITY OF THE 21ST CENTURY

Wherever it is that we learned to fear change, there is no reason for it. We are masters of change. Whenever it was that we lost our childlike enthusiasm and sense of the inexhaustible possibilities of life, there is no reason to continue in that vein today. Can you remember the thrill and excitement you felt as a small child, considering the endless numbers of ideas for what you would do when you grew up? The choices were so many and you wanted to choose them all, today a firefighter, tomorrow a nurse, the next day a teacher. The possibilities remain endless and stretch before us as far and as wide as the mind's eye can explore. Whatever age you are and wherever you are in your career, if an outdated perspective no longer serves your purposes, consider a new one.

6

The Only Two Tools You Will Ever Need

Human beings do not live in the objective world alone, nor alone in the world of social activity as ordinarily understood, but are very much at the mercy of the particular language which has become the medium of expression for their society. It is quite an illusion to imagine that one adjusts to reality essentially without the use of language and that language is merely an incidental means of solving specific problems of communication or reflection. The fact of the matter is that the "real world" is to a large extent unconsciously built up on the language habits of the group...We see and hear and otherwise experience very largely as we do because the language habits of our community predispose certain choices of interpretation.

. . . B.L. WHORF, *Language, Thought, and Reality,* 1956

LANGUAGE IS LEVERAGE

We have seen how personal perspectives and mindsets determine our reality. This chapter shows how to put that insight to practical use to create

a richer, more meaningful working life. Basically, only two tools are required, the two components of communication—listening and speaking.
But to understand this, we need to be clear that the 21st-century definition of communication is vastly different from its 20th-century meaning.
To illustrate, consider the story of Brenda.

Tom has long been in search of a special telephone, one designed
to look like an early 20th-century country store model, wood with two
brass bells on the front. Walking past the AT&T retail phone store in the
Fox Run Mall he sees, on display, the exact model he has been dream-
ing about, priced at $99.00. He walks up to the counter and meets
Brenda. Unbeknownst to Tom, Brenda has just learned that her store
and all the other AT&T phone stores across the nation are to be shut
down next week, as part of a 40,000 person downsizing. Naively, Tom
asks about the phone hanging on the wall. *No. I'm sorry. They are closing
down all the AT&T stores across the country next week. We're not taking any
orders. I don't know what I am going to do. How could they do this to us?* She
bursts into tears.

Later that afternoon, Tom walks into one of the new home improvement superstores across the street from the mall. On the end cap of the
home communications aisle sits a stack of country store phones (identical
to the AT&T model) for $49.95. On the door of the superstore is a large
"Help Wanted" sign. But Brenda, through her tears, cannot see the sign.

The first thing to notice about this story is that a communication
from headquarters has shifted Brenda's reality. The message is not one of
information, not like a weather report or a football score. It is a message
that directly alters her circumstances—she and 40,000 others are going
to be fired. Whoever spoke the message is altering reality just as powerfully as if they set off a bomb.

Twentieth-century thinking places the responsibility on circumstances, not on people. *Markets have changed, so action was necessary. The
corporate strategy dictates changes. In the interests of the shareholders, it has
become obvious....* In 21st-century thinking, these passive-voice, imper-
sonal statements are a smoke screen. The fact is that someone decided
to fire Brenda, spoke those words, and now she is history. Whether the
decision is good or bad, just or unjust, competent or incompetent, it is
a decision someone makes and speaks. Corporations being what they

are, the spoken message is passed along through layers of people. If Brenda asks her manager who fired her or why, he will only point to a directive from the next layer. In other words, in 20th-century tradition, the manager is simply passing along information.

Sometimes, of course, people do not simply pass along information, rather they take a stand on the information itself. President Nixon, under investigation for alleged Watergate crimes, ordered his attorney general, Elliot Richardson, to fire special prosecutor Archibald Cox. Richardson refused.

If people take responsibility for what they say, the 21st century will be noble.

Mark is the manager of a manufacturing plant. The plant produces, among other things, most of the world's most popular breakfast cereal. His engineers have told him that, to remain competitive, he must introduce new automation into his packaging assembly lines. Corporate strongly supports this, and the department managers unanimously believe it is the best direction. All of them agree the automation will eliminate 15 percent of the jobs in the plant and produce significant cost savings. Many plant managers, facing such recommendations, might insist upon good treatment for the employees who will lose their jobs. Mark, however, goes a giant leap beyond that and says, publicly, *I commit that there will be no involuntary job loss from this automation project.* We will see later how such ennobling commitments enroll people and conjure up support and resources in a way never available to people who simply pass along the information.

In Brenda's case notice how she reacts, how she listens. The way in which she hears the message incapacitates her, disempowers her, and blinds her to new worlds of opportunity as close as just across the street. The Fox Run Mall, where she works, is in the midst of a region of prosperity. Every fifth store has a help-wanted sign, not just the home improvement center across the street. But Brenda has been conditioned to feel that losing a job, even with a company so out of touch with its customers that it charges twice what the competition does, is the end of the world.

Twentieth-century thinking tells us that reality is objective, external to us. The role of communication, therefore, is to share information with one another about that reality. Reality happens, so we just comment upon it, and pass along the information. *Something happened to the market, so it is necessary to lay people off. It is no one's fault, no one's responsibility, that is just the way it is.*

By contrast, 21st-century thinking holds there is no reality independent of the way we communicate about it. We listen to and perceive events, not as events themselves, but rather colored, filtered, and fundamentally reinterpreted to fit our perspective. The core, practical insight of 21st-century thinking is that our perspectives are themselves linguistic—we create and perpetuate our reality by how we choose to communicate, that is, how we choose to speak and listen to each other.

Language creates reality.

In other words, we alter human reality every time we speak. Equally, we create our own reality by how we listen and label. The implications are profound. If we could somehow change our speaking and listening, reality would shift dramatically. What appeared as problems would dissolve into irrelevance, and what appeared as impossible and unknowable would become simple and obvious.

When someone says *You're fired*, it is easy to see how their speaking has shifted reality. But less obviously this same effect, this same shift, takes place whenever we say anything at all. To take a simple example, think about the object in your shirt pocket. What is it? A pen, you say. Before we mentioned it here in the book, you were probably not thinking about your pen at all. Now you are. Thus the act of naming has changed something in your perceived reality—it pulls an object out of the undifferentiated void and allows you to be aware of it, to use it as a tool.

But what if you chose a different label? Called something different, your pen could be instead a pointer, a toy, a status symbol (especially if yours is a Mont Blanc pen), a weapon, something to throw at the cat to discourage him from clawing the sofa, a conductor's baton, an ear-cleaning device, a coffee stirrer, a letter opener, a device to push the buttons on your telephone, a representation of the number 1, and a symbol of literacy.

Moving from pens to people, we see the same underlying structure in the way language creates reality. Have you ever felt pigeon holed in your job by your title? It makes a tremendous difference at a business meeting with strangers whether you are introduced as a secretary or a vice president. The label shifts completely how people treat you and how seriously they take your ideas. You can experiment with this yourself, the next time you are at a business meeting with people who do not know you. If you are a vice president, introduce yourself as a secretary, and watch what happens to the respect and attentiveness that you usually enjoy. Conversely, if you are a secretary, go to a meeting where you are not known, and introduce yourself as the vice president.

20th- and 21st-Century Language

But perhaps you object that the object in your pocket is *really* a pen. If so, where did it get that identity, that label? The pen itself has no knowledge of itself as a pen. Its being a pen is not something that it generated by itself. So how did it get its identity?

What if, when we label an object, we create it. That creation, as in calling the object a "pen," gives us access to it, allows us to perceive it, use it, and manipulate it, and communicate about it with our friends. At the same time, labeling the object also limits it—it prevents it from being all the other things it might be, as in the example. Twentieth-century thinkers ascribe this power of naming to some source outside themselves—the pen is a pen because it says so in the dictionary, because my mother taught me that it was, or because that's just the way it is. Twenty-first-century thinkers make *themselves* the authority, and the "pen" becomes a "pointer" because you are open to new possibilities for what things might be and because you said so.

Fixed identities of objects—from pens to people—cast in linguistic stone, are a hallmark of 20th-century thinking. Fluid identity signals 21st-century thinking. One practical result is that under a 21st-century model, you consider people and ideas on their own merits, rather than filtering them based on whatever label they happen to have. An example of this shift is that the stigma once attached to being laid off is disappearing. Until recently, being laid off was a shameful matter that would seriously hurt your chances for a new position. In other words, employers would evaluate you, not on the basis of whether you were a good fit for the job, but rather on the basis of whether you had the label *laid off* attached to you. Today, with layoffs so widespread and capricious, that particular prejudice is disappearing.

This fluidity produces surprising and creative results. For example, after hearing these ideas, the manager of one plant realizes the need for a crucial new function, one that does not exist in the traditional organization charts. This function, for which there is no name yet, maintains and directs positive and constructive interactions between workers and management—not just mediating disputes or papering over problems, but harnessing the power of creative interactions and applying that power to solving problems such as scheduling, improving plant efficiency, and reducing waste. In a move unprecedented in the history of the plant, he offers this position to an assembly-line worker—someone with years of plant experience who also happens to have an inquiring mind and a gift for helping people work better together.

The 21st-century will see many changes in all aspects of life. But the most fundamental and far reaching will be constant change in our perspective on reality itself, as reflected in our axioms of thinking, in how we speak, and in how we listen. Fluid thinking and free categories give a greater scope for growth, innovation, and new possibilities. This freedom, this openness to reinterpretation, is essential if people are to thrive on change. In the late 20th century an astounding number of people, who thought they were locked into predictable and certain careers, found themselves downsized, laid off, and reengineered. The first and foremost obstacle they face is their definition of themselves. *I was addicted to the corporate culture,* bemoans a laid-off geologist. *Employees Anxious As Layoffs Looms*, reads a NEW YORK TIMES headline on the eve of a 40,000 job cutback.[1] But why is not knowing an agony? *Most people need*

---

[1]"Employees Anxious As Layoffs Looms," by Robert Hanley, *New York Times*, January 4, 1996, p. D3.

a structured, organized environment, explains a personnel director. Let us hope his statement is not a universal truth about people. The 21st century will be many things, but it will not be structured and organized. If most people need structure, then most people will not be able to live in the 21st century. Could it be, though, that *most people need structure* is a statement similar to *this is a pencil*, true only because someone said so and subject to change and reinterpretation by free-thinking people?

Commitments and Consequences

Assuming that we have some choice in the matter of our perspectives, what perspectives would we choose to employ? Why, if we could, would we choose one perspective over another, and what would be the consequences? There is no more important decision that any of us can make because our perspective determines every aspect of our reality— what opportunities we can see, whether or not we will be happy in any circumstance, what success is for us, and how we will pursue it.

In retrospect, the 20th century was an era whose dominant value was control, the bottom line, and getting to the point. People sought control, not just of nature or of other people, but more deeply, control over control itself, that is, control over reality. Any endeavor that increased control was valued and any endeavor that decreased control was suspect. The goal of 20th-century science, for example, is prediction and control. Twentieth-century psychology strives to control and predict people. Twentieth-century biology seeks to control disease and even the genetic basis of life itself. Such control makes it possible to preselect your children's sex or to screen you for a job based on your genetic makeup. Similarly, the core value of large 20th-century corporations has been profits and the bottom line. This core value produced a perspective, a mental filter, in the listening of executives.

Increasingly, though, we are realizing that personal perspectives based on control as a core value have their limits and may even backfire. Sex selection in the third world, where boys are preferred to girls, would produce serious and far-reaching population imbalances. Genetic screening could produce social upheaval, even revolution. Many antibiotics, say experts, are coming to the end of their useful lives. Even worse, overuse of these medicines has produced resistant strains of bacteria more virulent and harder to treat than pre-antibiotic strains ever were. Meanwhile, our efforts to control the environment have drastically reduced the biological pool of available life forms from which we might have discovered new disease-treating agents.

In business, it is clear that control-oriented management contains the seeds of its own undermining. Control defeats the very purpose it was designed to fulfill. The end result of the era of the bottom line is that the largest 20th-century companies are all shrinking as we approach the end of the century. As a group, the Fortune 500 has fewer employees and controls a smaller share of the total economic pie in the mid-nineties than it did in the previous decade.

Twenty-first-century thinking approaches the problem of getting along in the world in an entirely different way. Fundamentally, it values freedom, creativity, and new possibilities. Instead of attempting to increase predictability, it capitalizes on chaos, unpredictability, and diversity. Brenda, the (former) AT&T retail phone store employee now has, if she chooses to exploit it, a much freer, more wide-open future than she had before the downsizing. Before, she was going to remain a phone store clerk indefinitely. Now she has literally thousands of career possibilities and opportunities to explore. There are entire peoples throughout human history who were willing to give up everything they had in exchange for a fraction of the freedom Brenda now enjoys.

If the 21st is to be a century of freedom, possibility, and constructive chaos, what tools are most appropriate for succeeding at work? Put simply, the ability to spot opportunities and the ability to market yourself—to listen and, once you have mastered listening, to speak.

21ST-CENTURY COMMUNICATION SKILLS

Productive Listening

You already know how to listen in a way that limits. Here is a simple but powerful exercise to prove that. Ask a friend to do the exercise with you. Ask your friend to speak to you extemporaneously for two minutes about some subject that deeply interests or excites him or her. The subject could be a favorite hobby, their career, their political views, or their hottest new workplace proposal. Your job is to listen with complete disinterest. Make it obvious that you are bored, and have your mind on something else. You can try looking away, reading the newspaper, yawning, and shaking your head and muttering to yourself, or even walking out of the room. You may wish to explain ahead of time what you are doing, else you are apt to lose a friend.

People cannot speak if no one listens.

Now try the exercise again, asking your partner to speak once more about a favorite topic, the same one as before, or something else. This time, pay rapt attention. Look your partner in the eye, smile and nod, and show by your every expression that you find their presentation fascinating.

Now ask your partner what the two experiences were like and how they compared to each other. He or she will tell you that it is almost impossible to sustain any enthusiasm in their speaking while you are feigning disinterest. They get upset with you and lose their flow of creative ideas. Perhaps they even begin to doubt their own interest in the topic. By contrast, they will tell you that when you pay attention they feel supported, creative, and have more to say.

To experience this for yourself, switch roles with your partner. Now you speak about something you care about, while your partner shows disdain. Notice what it feels like, what it does to your confidence and ability to express yourself. Notice how much easier it is to be creative and enthusiastic about your topic when your partner is interested and supportive.

This simple exercise shows the profound effect that listening has on people's ability to speak. It really is worthwhile to try the exercise, for it will make the importance of listening unforgettable for you. You cannot speak effectively when there is no listening for what you have to say. Or put another way, if you do not provide a generous listening for those important to you, they cannot speak to you.

If you did the exercise, you know about one kind of listening—listening with disinterest—and how profoundly that limits communication.

Conversely, you now know a more productive way to listen, that generates better communication.

Altering our listening is a skill not much practiced in the 20th century. As citizens of that mechanistic world, we have been taught that our listening is neutral. It can be a shock to learn we have the freedom to choose what we hear and that how we choose to listen affects the message at its source. It is easier to run on auto pilot, delegate the responsibility for what we hear to the speaker, and expect him or her to transform our hearing without accommodation from us.

For the 21st century, we invite you to create your life and your destiny, beginning completely anew. And what would you like to create for yourself, your family, and your co-workers? How would you like it to be? Challenge every assumption. Would you like to work fewer hours? Would you like the work to be more human, more relationship centered than related to machine? Would you like to tune into the extraordinary possibilities in corporate shrinkage, reengineering, and downsizing? What would it mean to have a great day at work, one day at a time?

There are other kinds of listening, presented next, that can help achieve all these and other goals. Although we contrast each with a 20th-century form of listening, none are simple modifications or translations. The contrast is more radical since, viewed or used from a 20th-century framework, these new forms of listening tend to obscure. All depend on a fundamental shift of perspective to the view that communication does not reflect reality but rather creates it.

Listening for Possibility

In 1993, Marcus Wilson is named a vice president at Intel Corporation. But in 1973 Marcus is just starting his career. He has landed a job with Texas Instruments as a calculator salesman. He is sent to Florida to report to the sales manager there. As junior man, he is given an unpromising territory—Miami. Calculator sales there are among the lowest in the country, and it soon becomes clear to Marcus that his manager expects little of him.

A few trips to the major department stores and electronics shops produce unpromising results. But Marcus knows how to listen for possibility, how to think outside traditional boundaries. In looking for outlets, he notices that in Miami there are discount department stores that cater to the Hispanic community. Though enormous, they are not part of national chains. These stores are located on the second floors of warehouses and do not have signs. They advertise in the Spanish newspapers so a non-Spanish speaker would probably not be aware of them. But the Hispanic community are loyal customers and come in droves. Not only that, but these stores are known throughout South America so that when South Americans make a visit to Miami one of the highlights is a trip to the Hispanic discount stores.

Texas Instruments and the Florida sales manager have never heard of these outlets and are skeptical. But Marcus gets the idea to approach them. At first suspicious, the store managers soon learn to trust him and place some orders. The calculators sell like hot cakes. Within six months, the Miami sales district is the highest performing in the nation.

Listening for possibility, listening outside the realm of the expected and the established, may be the most essential skill for success in the 21st century. To cultivate it, develop the habit of playing with ideas. Spin out scenarios and possibilities in your mind without regard to their seeming practicality. Be open to the unexpected and the creative.

Twentieth-century thinkers have difficulty with the idea of possibility. It seems insubstantial, unreal, and divorced from hard, businesslike goals. Progress is made by ferocious focus. Twenty-first-century thinking views these strengths as weaknesses. Focus produces blindness, not results. The possible, that which could-be but is-not-yet, is the raw material of creative progress. The 21st-century skill of listening for possibility uses an initially fluid and free-form approach to expand the range of solutions before homing in on a specific result.

For example, when people look for a new house, they usually start with a specific list of requirements. Realtors report that the biggest obstacle to helping people find a house they would really love is the buyers' preconceptions—what they think they are looking for before they ever see a house.

On some fortunate occasions, however, and perhaps in your own experience, the house the buyers end up with may be strikingly different and far more satisfying than the one that they originally specify. One couple starts out looking for a modern split level and ends up buying a

200-year-old colonial. They have no experience with old colonials and it has never entered their minds even to consider one. But the minute they see it, they fall in love. If they had insisted on looking only at split-levels, they could never have had that delightful result.

The trick, the difference, has to do with how you approach the house-buying experience. In one approach, you make up a list of requirements beforehand. Then you rank every house on how well it fits the requirements. Since all houses always fall short, the final decision is always a compromise. The alternative approach is to view each house newly, without preconception, and to imagine yourself living there. The goal, at this point, is not to decide about the house, but simply to have the experience, at least in imagination, of actually living in it. Then, if you find the experience delightful, you can buy the house.

This opening up to new possibilities without, at least initially, a specific and preplanned result in mind, is at the heart of the 21st-century idea of listening. What the idea lacks in initial focus, it more than makes up for in ultimate possibility.

Listening against a fixed set of preconceptions is appropriate only if your preconceptions are an accurate and exhaustive model of the world. Perhaps, in times of stasis, some people's preconceptions form a perfect model of the world, and fixed listening serves them well. However, in a constantly changing environment, preconceptions will never fit the situation. Instead of trying to force the world to fit the preconceptions, the 21st-century alternative is to be open to whatever the new world has to offer. Two couples move from New England to Arizona. Both are avid gardeners. One couple tries to recreate a New England garden—lush green lawns, deciduous trees, and familiar flowers. The result is an expensive, high maintenance eyesore which withers in the 120-degree heat. The second couple, open to the new possibilities of desert gardening, creates an exotic paradise of cacti and Mexican bird-of-paradise bushes.

In times of constant change, the value of serendipitous and unexpected results outweighs the value of planned achievements.

Listening for Unexpected Opportunity

The 20th-century world is a world ruled by cause-and-effect. We generalize this limited law of physics even to human affairs, notwithstanding that human affairs have multiple, even chaotic, causes. For example, have you noticed that every weekday evening, the nightly business news gives a simple reason as to why the stock market went up or down? Yesterday, for instance, the Dow was up 75 points. The reason given was that President Clinton and House Speaker Gingrich were willing to talk about avoiding another government shutdown. But it turns out that these reasons are made up after the fact by someone who works for the wire service! No one really has any idea why the market goes up or down (or if anyone does they are not about to tell the world). Besides, the reason changes each day. But our listening for cause-and-effect is so insistent that we must have a simple reason (a cause) even for inherently chaotic and inexplicable events! Woe betide the investor who takes these reasons seriously. Today, President Clinton and House Speaker Gingrich are still willing to talk to each other, but the market is down.

Cause-and-effect analysis works well to predict the behavior of two billiard balls on a pool table. But it fails to predict even situations that involve as few as three billiard balls (the three-body problem). There are not enough basic laws in the physics of motion to handle such a situation. Nonetheless, we approach problems of infinitely greater complexity as though they can be explained and manipulated by a single cause. For example, in the latter part of the century, the corporate problem is to boost profits. What causes lack of profits? Having to pay wages and salaries, of course. So hundreds of thousands of people are let go. Later, the American Management Association comes out with the "surprising" report that most of the companies who downsized have failed to boost profits and furthermore, now suffer from poor morale.

Listening for cause-and-effect, for simple single causes, is invariably misleading and usually dangerous.

The 21st-century alternative to cause-and-effect based listening is listening for unexpected opportunity. This form of listening does not presuppose that the world progresses by simple, predictable, mechanistic laws, but rather is in a constant state of flux and chaos. The unexpected is always happening. Instead of trying to minimize or control it, the trick is to be open to the unexpected, even if how it happens appears to run counter to our orderly predictive models of the way things should be.

For example, at a food manufacturing plant, corporate announces a new policy that employees may not wear wedding rings, other than plain bands, on the food packing lines. Even the minute chance of stones ending up in the food and breaking a child's tooth is too great a risk. A disgruntled employee calls the local TV station and the possibility of a major negative news item looms ominously. The manager is concerned about the impact unfavorable press will have on corporate's already jaundiced view of this facility. Instead of listening to his old model that the union committee chairman is a troublemaker who will only make things worse, the manager decides to ask for his help. Pleased to be included in the loop, the union chairman speaks to employees throughout the plant and finds that the overwhelming majority understand and support the company policy. So he works to get TV interviews with employees who represent the majority view. *Yes, we care about the safety and purity of our products. After all, a wedding band is only a symbol—what makes a marriage is how people treat each other.* These positive comments are not in the least newsworthy, so the news item disappears, literally overnight. This instance of positive cooperation radically shifts both the manager's and the committee chairman's views of each other, making additional productive collaborations possible.

Another dynamic example occurs at a school district during contract negotiations. The teachers and central administration are meeting to consider the possibility of extending the existing contract. An extension will give them much-needed time to improve their relationship, which has deteriorated over several years. The two sides are close to an agreement but cannot come to terms. Then, the superintendent walks in, listens to the issues, and over the objections of his negotiating team, agrees to the teachers' requests. He makes it clear that he cares about the teachers and wants them to receive the best treatment possible. This act is entirely out of the norm for him and it turns the relationship around. The negotiators for the teachers, instead of listening for the cause, the why, the hidden agenda behind what the superintendent says, seize the moment, take the man at his word, and agree to the extension.

Listening with Gratitude

Gratitude is out of fashion in the late 20th century. This is a shame because gratitude is fundamental to the successful pursuit of happiness.

Twentieth-century thinking holds that whatever is of value in life is of necessity scarce and so must be husbanded, rationed, and defended. Twenty-first-century thinking holds that scarcity is a made-up myth and that the really important things in life are available in abundance, because they can be created at will and in infinite amounts by people.

> Scarcity is a myth.

In a corporation undergoing upheaval, with declining revenues and job losses on the horizon, Peter Conklin, the program manager, gives a workshop for a product-development group. Group members discuss their fears about the future. Peter has them make a list of things they are afraid of. Fear of losing their jobs comes out higher than the fear of death! *Do you realize,* he says, *that whatever happens, you are always going to have enough to eat?* They look confused. *Yes, in this society, you will never go hungry,* says Peter. Throughout most of human history, and even today for the majority of the human race, the news that they will never be hungry would be a miracle, a cause for fantastic celebration. But the product-development group only looks glum.

If you listen without gratitude, it does not matter what you have enough of. There will always be something else that you will construe as scarce. Food is something the product-development group takes for granted. They want something more. Yet, if they were guaranteed that, they would want even more of whatever seems scarce next, and so on forever.

One of the most striking traits many people exhibit after they have been laid off is bitterness. However satisfying or even justified, it is strongly self-defeating. Bitterness blinds us to the good that has happened and to the good yet to come. Bitterness is also highly repellent to others, especially job interviewers. When someone is let go after 20 years, must the reaction be one of having been shafted? Might it be possible to be appreciative for the 20 years, sad that they are over, and excited about life's next adventure?

Listening for Value

Twentieth-century listening filters everything through a sieve of prior judgments and fixed opinions and rejects everything that does not conform to existing prejudice. To see an extreme example, tune into CSPAN when proceedings in the House of Representatives are being televised. There you can see legislators giving impassioned speeches to their colleagues who are not listening at all. Often, no one is even in the audience; the speaker addresses an empty chamber. Other times, the audience is there but they are talking among themselves, walking up and down the aisles, or working on their papers. Apparently the other members have decided beforehand that the speaker cannot possibly have anything of value to say, so they pay no attention. The speeches become an empty facade, a masquerade, and the meaning and possibility of reasoned legislative dialog and inquiry are lost. This high-level nonlistening sets the worst possible example for the rest of the national community. Our politicians' lack of listening skills may explain much voter disenchantment and apathy. If legislators will not listen even to each other, why should anyone else listen to them?

In extreme contrast, the National Issues Convention is, in 1996, an experiment in what it takes to generate productive political dialog. This brainchild of political science professor James Fishkin creates a setting for 600 private citizens, randomly chosen from across the United States, to come, all expenses paid, to Austin, Texas, for a week of productive dialog. The people break into teams to learn from experts and get to know each other before having a chance to interview the presidential candidates on national television. Fishkin and his colleagues succeed in creating a climate conducive to listening for value. For example, Mike, from the tiny town of Fowler, Michigan, has a chance to meet Valerie who lives in a town where crack cocaine is sold on every other corner. The encounter changes his mind about drug-enforcement policy and funding. Similarly dramatic shifts of opinion on many issues are common across the entire 600-person convention. This experiment shows that when people actually listen to each other, they learn new perspectives and information and change their minds.

Every human being has something to teach us.

Listening for value means tuning into the lesson each person we meet has to offer. Ordinarily, our tendency to listen in terms of *I am right and you are wrong* makes this way of listening impossible, and we cut ourselves off from the single most powerful source of ideas for improvement and change that we have available.

Listening for value is the opposite of listening for what is right and wrong about what another person says. Listening for value assumes that what the other person says is valid from his or her perspective, and that it has contextual coherence and legitimacy. The listener for value considers how the world appears for the speaker and acknowledges the validity of the viewpoint being expressed. This does not necessarily imply agreement. Validity and agreement are not the same. Agreement says, *Yes, that is my view also.* Validation says, *Yes, I can see what you are saying.*

Another way to practice listening for value is to focus, not on what is wrong, but rather on what is missing, which, if it were present, would make a positive difference. This removes the element of blame. For example, plant safety is an area in which it would be easy to listen for what is wrong, and to cast blame, especially when a worker is crushed to death on the loading dock, so hard that his glasses are embedded in the concrete. But one supervisor creates a safety program based on the idea of listening for value. This simple change of perspective has him listen for the lesson in whatever happens. He constantly asks, *What made you do that? Why did you make an unsafe choice? Why did you make a safe choice?* in response to incidents real or imagined. He is looking for underlying insights, not pointing fingers at his co-workers. As a consequence they are helpful and open, and actively contribute to safety in all its aspects. The program wins national awards and OSHA recognition as a model program. Listening for value in what others have to say is key to their active and enthusiastic participation.

Listening to How Others Listen

This form of 21st-century listening is so crucial to creating connections in a fluid, free-form work world that all of Chapter 7 (CREATE POWERFUL CONNECTIONS) is devoted to listening for others' perspectives. By way of brief preview, it is a way of listening behind what others are saying to experience the world as they perceive it. According to 21st-century thinking, the world is neither fixed nor objective. Rather it is constructed uniquely by each individual. Consequently, you cannot communicate effectively with anyone unless you have some appreciation for their unique world. The skill of listening to how others listen gives that appreciation.

Speaking that Makes a Difference

Communication consists of two completely intertwined activities, listening and speaking. Of the two, 90 percent of the leverage is in listening. If you learn to listen in the ways we suggest and invent others, your speaking will automatically become more powerful and impactful.

However, the core 21st-century insight that *communication creates reality* can inform your speaking and radically empower your communication skills. The 20th-century function of language is to comment on the world. The 21st-century function of language is to create the world.

There is a story about three umpires: an apprentice, a journeyman, and a seasoned veteran of the game. When questioned about their skill and accuracy at calling the plays, the apprentice speaks with assurance, *I calls them like they are!* The journeyman has greater insight and says, *I calls them like I see them.* The veteran, however, is wise and says, *They ain't nothin' till I calls them!*

The wise umpire realizes that speaking creates reality. As you may have seen for yourself in sports, what actually happens over the plate is of no consequence. The only thing that makes any difference to the score is the umpire's call. Other examples of the same phenomenon are when the jury foreman reads the verdict, when you speak the marriage vow at the altar, or when the president declares war. In all these cases, the spoken words do not describe, they create.

Twentieth-century thinking, with its focus on external, objective reality, relegates speaking to the passive, ineffectual role of commenting upon situations and passing judgment. Consider the barrage of assessments and complaints that comprise most social chitchat. Such conversations never change the world but serve only to reinforce *how bad things are*.

Which technique do you employ in your life? Are you a reporter of events or a creator of life? How do you listen to the news? To your co-workers? To your children? Do you create a great life here and now or bemoan the circumstances in which you find yourself?

Speaking that Shifts How Others Listen

Often, you have a message that others are simply not ready to hear. In such cases, it is critical to shift the way in which people are listening before you try to get the message across.

Jim Myers is an affable yet shrewd and experienced investment banker. One day he travels to make a presentation to the board of directors of a major corporation. He walks in, late in the day, for his scheduled appointment. He sees immediately that the board members, movers and shakers all, are at that hour, grumpy, petulant, and in no mood to listen to anything. *Great*, he thinks, *I've flown 2000 miles for this!* He sits and listens for a moment. The exhausted power brokers are at the end of a tiresome day of overly polished pitches and presentations, none of which have apparently impressed them. Jim sees there is no point at all in launching into his presentation. So instead, he fumbles distractedly for a moment and pulls out his wallet. *I have some pictures of my wife and kids here that I'd like you to see*, and he passes his photos around. Scowling at first, the grumpy potentates look at the pictures. After a few moments, one of the board members says, *I have some pictures I'd like to show too.* Soon everyone is exchanging photos of their families. The mood in the room completely alters and shortly Jim is able to begin his presentation, which is a success.

A word of warning. This exact strategy, showing pictures of your family, is unlikely to work for you in a similar situation. The genius of it is that Jim invents it on the spur of the moment. However, the general principle of recognizing when you need to change the message, plus the skill of listening to where others are coming from, will allow you to create a similar stroke of genius on the spur of your own moment.

Jim Myers' actions also show that speaking does not have to be verbal. Showing pictures, indeed any action to which people attach meaning, is a form of speaking.

Another way to change how others listen to you involves creating a new distinction, a new insight or framework. This is not just giving new information. By giving a new perspective you give your audience a new way to interpret information.

At a plant with a history of difficult labor-management relations, people have long memories and constantly rehash old war stories and grievances about how difficult the past has been. No one expects anything to change. Against this backdrop, the head of the union calls the committee members and stewards together for a special meeting. His words are simple and to the point when he tells his people that they must not hold the new managers responsible for what the prior managers have said or done. He tells them to allow the past to die and to create a new relationship with the current managers. A remarkable new working relationship begins between union and management, propelling the plant from the cellar to number one in productivity, profits, morale, safety, and efficiency.

Speaking that Creates the Future

I commit that there will be no involuntary job loss from this automation project.

So speaks Mark, a plant manager. His speaking has nothing to do with reporting information, stating opinions, or passing along policy. His declaration is a rare example of a man putting himself on the line and taking a stand. Making yourself responsible for an outcome is the only kind of speaking that makes any difference in human affairs.

Mark has no idea how to do this. Historical evidence is all against him. Automation in manufacturing, with attendant loss of jobs, has been going on for decades, both in his company and worldwide. Even the union has given up trying to stop job loss and contents itself with assuring good positions for those left after downsizing. When Mark first says this, no one responds or reacts in any visible way. The managers and the union leaders simply cannot hear the significance of the words or of the commitment behind them. A noble idea, they think, but not really expected, called for, or possible. It takes another two or three months, and numerous repetitions of his commitment, for his management team and the union leadership to grasp the significance and the serious intent behind his words. Gradually at first, then with more momentum, people start to hear. The union chairman starts an initiative to find new jobs for people, ones that have heretofore been contracted out. Mark helps him. Working together, they build trust and achieve results. Before they realize it, a year has passed and there have been no job losses at all. Their cooperation sets a model for the other managers and union stewards. Grievances decline from 30 per month to one or two, or even zero. Productivity soars. Corporate notices and the CEO pays a special visit. All of a sudden management and union leadership find themselves collaborating on a plan to bring a distribution center to town, a step that will expand, not shrink, the workforce.

These developments depend on Mark's original, courageous declaration. There is no way to build the future other than for someone to take that bold first step of committing to it, before it is clear how it will come to pass.

Reluctance to commit to unreasonable goals is 20th-century thinking's most debilitating legacy. Reluctance and hesitation are built into the philosophy that places the source of the action outside of ourselves, so that we sit and wait until circumstances are right for us to act. Twenty-first-century thinking short-circuits this fallacy by placing the source of human progress where it belongs—in the creative, courageous efforts of human beings.

The limiting case of 20th-century thinking is the bureaucratic organization in which no one takes responsibility for anything outside a limited domain. Efficient? Maybe. But which company would you rather do business with? One where the employee says, *That's not my department,* or where she says, *I am here to serve you. Whatever your concern, I will either solve it or make sure that someone else, competent to handle it, does.*

WORDS SPEAK LOUDER THAN ACTIONS

Twentieth-century wisdom holds that actions speak louder than words. Twenty-first-century perspective takes the opposite view, maintaining that there is no such thing as action absent interpretation in language.

But, is the nitty gritty of business not the end result, closing the deal, and making the numbers? *Talk is cheap, it's the bottom line that matters*, according to conventional wisdom. Consider Mark's declaration that no one will involuntarily lose a job as a result of automation. Then, suppose the automation project is implemented and 50 people lose their jobs. Are the naysayers, the people who refused to support Mark's project, proven right? Were they astute to withhold their support because time proves he cannot keep his promise? And, does Mark's failure to keep his promise disprove the power of speaking?

We say not. Mark's project succeeds because the managers and workers around him suspend their disbelief and embrace his commitment to bring it to reality. They add the power of their speaking to Mark's speaking. For example, the head of the local union talks to personnel about in-house employees doing contract work. The managers make sure corporate knows that grievances are down. The project catches fire, people get involved, and each does what she or he can.

If the converse comes to pass—Mark's project fails—is it possible that a lack of support in the form of negative speaking from the people around him is the source of the failure? In 20th-century thinking, we make a judgment and then feel justified when our judgment comes true. *Oh, that will never succeed. No one can possibly do that.* But consider these statements from a 21st-century perspective. Was there a time in your own experience—there certainly was in ours—when you passed a negative assessment or judgment on someone else's initiative, and it indeed failed? Is it possible that your lack of support lay at the heart of the failure?

Objective thinkers do not understand this distinction. *The facts show that America is no longer the land of opportunity*, proclaims a prestigious research institute across headlines, radio, and television. Their objective research is laced with statistics about declining job opportunities.

But consider. Does their statement reflect reality or create it? A declining number of jobs may be a fact. But to say that America is no longer the land of opportunity is a destructive interpretation masquerading as a fact. What makes America the land of opportunity is only one thing—the belief of all the world that it is so.

Speaking creates reality. What you say is what you get. So say it.

Part III
Tools for 21st-Century Work

If we are to achieve results
Never before accomplished
We must expect to employ methods
Never before attempted.

. . . SIR FRANCIS BACON, *Essays*, 1625

7

Create Powerful Connections

America's best buy is a telephone call to the right man.

ILKA CHASE

WHY CONNECT?

If you are fortunate, you will have many different jobs and explore many business opportunities in your lifetime. This means that you will meet many more people than you otherwise would have, people from backgrounds, cultures, and experiences unfamiliar to you. That being so, one of the most important 21st-century skills will be the ability to get along with a lot of different kinds of people. You will want skills to quickly understand where other people are coming from, how they think, what is of value to them, what will appeal to them, and how the world looks to them. It will serve you well to be open and flexible, able to see the mutual benefit in even the most unlikely partnerships. This chapter presents a framework and way of thinking to make you a master at genuine connection.

> Nothing, absolutely nothing, will be more important to you in the 21st-century workplace than your genuine connections.

TRANSCENDING 20TH-CENTURY ISOLATION

The 20th-century organization, hierarchical and divided, often discourages or even prevents winning connections between people of different backgrounds. Dividing work into functions, such as manufacturing, engineering, marketing, sales, personnel, and R&D can isolate people with differing perspectives and talents. This isolation cuts off productive and creative interaction and limits a company's possibilities. For example, one mega-corporation, following a common model, strictly divides engineering and sales. The vice president of sales announces that his strategy is to build a wall around his division. He does so by leasing offices that are separate from the engineering plants in different parts of the country. He negotiates an entirely different compensation and benefits structure. He even installs computer communications that are deliberately incompatible with the engineering networks. His plan, over the years, works. Virtually no one in engineering even knows, let alone talks with, anyone in sales. Over time, the rank and file in each camp develop a negative mythology about each other. Engineers and salespeople become *propeller heads* and *sleaze artists* to one another. Sometimes, though, a customer asks to see an engineer, to learn what the product is actually designed to do. The salespeople, who by now speak a completely different language from the engineers, try to find someone. Their messages are written in what appears to the engineers as strange jargon. Engineering finds someone it thinks is appropriate, and sales flies her off to the customer in India, or Japan. But when the far-flung meeting happens, it turns out that the engineer's specialty has nothing whatsoever to do with what the customer wanted, and the meeting is an expensive fiasco.

By contrast, Volvo Car Corporation makes a successful experiment in cross-functional collaboration. Starting from the idea of delivering better sales and service to the customer, the company initiates a program whereby car salespeople and software engineers collaborate to create an on-line showroom. Together they design a system that lets the customer see their new Volvo, on a vivid, full-color computer screen. Want green with butternut leather seats? Click a button and see your new car in three dimensions. Want to see how it will look in your driveway? Scan in a photo and the system superimposes your car. Click and select the options you want, see them appear in the 3-D image, and see a table with price and financing terms, all computed in an instant. Happy with your choice? Click a button and the order is instantly sent to the factory in Gothenburg. The team that creates this consists of several Swedish Volvo showroom salesmen, not so different looking from their American counterparts except for the accent, and a group of young, enthusiastic Swedish software engineers. Neither knows much at all about each other's worlds. But they approach the collaboration with respect—the salespeople in awe of what the engineers can create, and the engineers in awe of the salespeople's knowledge of what will appeal to the customer. Their design is a success.

> Human progress depends on productive interaction between different cultures.

SCRIPTED AND GENUINE INTERACTIONS

Have you noticed that in your interactions with people, some could be called *scripted* while others are *genuine?* For example, Chase Manhattan, in the process of laying off 10,000 people as a result of a merger, sends to the firing managers a booklet of instructions on how to do the firing.[1] The guidelines are clear—plan meeting for 5-10 minutes. State that the person is let go. Be terse. Do not give any apology. If you fear an emotional outburst, alert security and medical. In a scripted conversation the purpose, content, and intended result are planned beforehand, and nothing the employee can say will change the outcome.

---

[1]"The Company as Family, No More," by N. R. Kleinfield, *New York Times*, March 4, 1996, p. 1 ff.

Scripted conversations produce predetermined outcomes.

The whole point of a scripted conversation is to act out a foregone conclusion. An obvious example is the telemarketer who races through the script without pausing for a breath, precisely to prevent any input from the listener. Con artists of all sorts devise clever scripts that masquerade as genuine, at least for a time. Whenever people choose to act out a role rather than behave as themselves, the conversation is scripted. The belief that we are paid only to play out some predefined pose dehumanizes the business world. For example, a manager at Chase Manhattan knows that he must lay off several people in his department next month. But before this happens, one of his people comes up to him for a friendly discussion in the hall. *I'm thinking of buying a house. Do you think it's a good idea?* The manager gets to decide whether to follow orders, reveal nothing about the impending layoffs, and let this man go ahead with his house purchase, or whether to warn him off from what will be an ill-timed move. He decides to follow the corporate script, deliberately deceiving his employee and friend. The man buys the house, gets laid off, and loses his house. Years later, the manager is still troubled over whether or not he did the right thing.

Without intending to deceive or to behave as robots, we all place tremendous value on preplanned conversations. We search for the secret, the perfect script that will get us what we want in our interactions with other people. We are attracted to lists of how-to, three steps to this, twelve steps to that. This is not surprising since we live in a 20th-century world that values and rewards prediction and control.

But, consider the deep and lasting relationships that result when people are thrown together in a traumatic experience. Tragedies of all kinds—the terrible experience of war, a death in a family, even the simple terror of being trapped in an elevator can strip people of the facade, allowing them to speak frankly and with sensitivity to one another. The tie between people that results from these experiences can remain vital for years as the veterans and survivors of every war will attest. What happens at these times is real, bona fide, ingenuous, and candid communication. People abandon their roles, titles, and position in society, listening and speaking to one another as people.

The key to genuine conversation is in the art of listening.

THE POWER OF GENUINE CONNECTION

Genuine conversation is spontaneous, with a natural and creative flow. In genuine conversation no one knows from the outset exactly what will be discussed or what the result will be. Both parties in a genuine conversation are open to new results. When you have a genuine conversation, there is a sense of connection, of rapport, of creating something together. This spirit stands out in the Volvo on-line showroom design team. Engineers and salesmen alike know, from their own experience together, that the really meaningful results, the breakthroughs, are always based on genuine interactions.

At the Fremont, New Hampshire annual town meeting, a citizen gets up to the microphone to address his fellow townspeople. Four hundred people fill the school gym, a record attendance for this town that has practiced this form of government and decision making for over 200 years. At issue today is whether this town of 2,000 souls should spend $80,000 to buy land on which to build a new fire and police station. The nervous citizen speaks of his love of the town, his heritage there, and the residents' responsibilities to one another. His words are halting and unrehearsed, yet they capture the imagination of the meeting. The purchase is approved.

Another powerful example of a genuine conversation occurs when Peter Conklin, then responsible for printer development at Digital Equipment Corporation, meets with the man responsible for the Alpha Project in its early stages. The Alpha Project, Digital's attempt to develop a 64-bit microprocessor, is the only hope for this company to save itself from final disintegration. Most analysts believe that, even if wildly successful, the product will be too little and far too late. Their meeting is not related to the project and, yet, as Peter tells it later, *Somewhere in our conversation, it became clear that there should be a program office for the Alpha Project and that I should be the head of that office. Later, neither of us knew from where that idea emerged. We just realized that we had a common vision and rapport.* As it happens, Peter is exactly the man for the job. He leads the project to success in the years that follow. Then, in May, 1995, just weeks before Digital announces profits from the Alpha chip, Peter has a massive heart attack and dies. Insiders know the enormity of his personal contribution to the reemergence of that company.

That contribution was possible owing to an open conversation between two men, both listening attentively and responding to whatever arose in the conversation. No one had considered the possibility of a project office before that day and, at the end of their meeting, the office and its director were in place.

We cannot know in advance the power of a single genuine conversation to change the future.

Twentieth-century thinking deludes us that we can win the day with powerful scripts, prepared beforehand. But what if it is actually the case that we become free and powerful when we throw away our prepared scripts and speeches and enter the world of ingenuous, in-the-moment, spontaneous conversation?

WORLDS TO EXPLORE

Throwing out the script gives us an opportunity to hear, *really hear*, what the other person is trying to communicate. The next step is to believe him. What he is saying is an expression of the world as he *knows* it to be. So often, we fail to realize that the other person speaks about the world *they* see, not the world *we* see. We think the other person dwells in the same world as we do. Nothing could be further from the truth. The world they inhabit and describe is theirs alone.

For example, at one manufacturing plant, several months after the union committee and the management have forged an effective working relationship, the numbers of grievances drop almost to zero. At a union-hall meeting, the business agent lambasts the committee members, *Everybody is so damn happy around here our members aren't getting taken care of. People have grievances and they aren't being filed. You should be filing more grievances.* At first glance you might wonder what the business agent is talking about. Is he trying to stir up trouble? No, he is conveying something that he sees. Plant employees have been calling the business agent at home to complain that their grievances are being ignored. To the business agent, it appears that employees' issues are not being resolved. He is not actually suggesting that the committee should simply file more grievances. Rather, the committee should verify that people's concerns are satisfied before a grievance is closed. Some of the committee members realize this and respond appropriately. At least one does not, and the result is a flurry of grievances from that department. Several weeks later the business agent observes that too many grievances are being written and wants to know what's wrong. He admonishes the committee to resolve, not escalate, employee complaints.

Each of us has our own internalized philosophy or personal perspective. Even when we are born and reared in the same country and culture, we see different things, experience emotions differently, and have different definitions of success and failure. We literally experience different realities. A simple demonstration of this can be drawn with the word *failure*. We think, because we speak the same language that we know what is meant by *failure*. Yet studies have shown that the meanings assigned to this word range from *If I fail I might as well fall on my sword and die* to *Failure is like missing a basket during practice.* You can imagine the consequences of lightly using the word *fail* with someone who believes failure is permanent and final.

Life is never dull and people are never boring. Diversities are a source of enrichment in our lives and work, especially as we learn to recognize and respond appropriately to them. The Volvo salespeople notice entirely different aspects of their environment than the Swedish software engineers—they live in different worlds.

Your job is to build bridges between the worlds.

Presented below are pictures of nine *operating worlds* or *perspectives* that you can expect to encounter frequently in business. Each perspective offers value and wisdom in both the professional and personal arenas. We are not suggesting these nine are exhaustive. You may find it exciting to look for others. Especially when a person says something that does not make sense to you, you may want to consider, *Now what does he see that causes him to say that?* When people speak they are, truly, describing a world that you cannot know. However, as you might do on tour to a foreign land, you can listen openly and attentively to discover as much of the terrain as possible, thus enriching your own experience and making possible valuable and productive connections with other people.

Before Reading the Next Nine Sections:

+ As you read, notice your reaction to the perspectives presented. What do you think of each perspective? (i.e., intelligent, sensible, illogical, silly, just like me.)
+ Do you know someone who favors each perspective? In what way do you now understand their perspective better?
+ Write a sentence or two about how you might persuade this person (or any person of this "persuasion") to come to work with you. What would you say to excite and entice them?

The World of Quality

You hire a contractor to convert your spare room into a home office. You show him your ideas and agree on a price. He sets to work. As the weeks roll by, you thrill to the care and craftsmanship. You want dark blue walls and varnished mahogany beams and you are delighted that each beam is finished off with exquisitely mitered moldings and that the switch plates are brass instead of plastic. A year later, you are amazed that the heating and air-conditioning bills are much lower than you expect. Your investigation reveals expertly installed insulation. Still later you discover that new appliances and equipment easily plug into the extra outlets and light fixtures. Lucky you! The contractor you hired is a proponent of quality.

In the world of quality there is an underlying conviction of a right way to do things. You might, yourself, have strong feelings about how something should be done especially if you are an expert on the subject. If you work with someone who has this underlying conviction, that there is exactly one way to properly discharge a job, you may think that you never have a voice in how things are done. A good way to appeal to someone with this frame of mind is to express the benefits for projects, financial or otherwise, in terms of *the right way to save money* or *laying the groundwork to insure things are done right in the future*. If this perspective is one you identify with personally, you may find that your relationships with others improve by reminding yourself, from time to time, that there are diverse ways to achieve the desired result.

For example, the distribution manager at a large manufacturing facility dedicates himself to turning around the attitude of the employees in his department. He wants them to own their jobs, always observing and recommending how to improve the processes, and reduce product damage. After several months, the department is functioning more efficiently, according to the bottom line, but the manager is not satisfied. He envisions an organization that runs smoothly, with few complaints, and where everyone works together cooperatively. His department seems to be always in an uproar and the employees are opinionated and strong willed about how the job should be done. Uproar does not fit his model of the way the department should operate. But then he realizes that his employees are thriving, taking ownership, and showing creativity. In his words, *The best way for me to hear is to listen from a neutral standpoint. (I) don't enter conversations from the stance of being right, but rather acknowledge the other person as being right as well.* As a consequence this manager enjoys his job a great deal more and the department is continuing to improve.

> A mature perspective toward quality and perfection knows when to lighten-up.

The World of Help and Mentoring

The proposal you made to the board has been rejected. Two years of careful preparation and hard work are down the drain. You are crushed, despondent. You call your mentor, an old, wise man, now confined to a wheelchair. He insists on hearing the unvarnished facts, restores your perspective and sense of yourself, and reminds you of your many assets and achievements. With his help, you formulate a bold new plan of action. You have entered the world of mentoring.

All of us support and help others, at least some of the time. You may work this way with your children or with a new employee who seems to be floundering. People who work for social service agencies often have this perspective. Some news reporting is designed to elicit the desire to help from the audience.

Most of us would love the opportunity to contribute to others. It is gratifying to be able to assist another person. Conversely, by asking for assistance when we ourselves need help, we are actually validating other people. To ask for help is a gift to the other person, and there is no better way to win an ally.

This perspective is at its best when it enables people to stretch and grow. For example, the vice president for operations of an underwear manufacturer makes radical changes in the work environment. The plants are located in rural areas, and the employees are primarily poorly educated women with little self-confidence. Some of them have been sewing the same seam in garment after garment, at a grueling piecework pace, for over a dozen years. They have extreme difficulty when they are expected to switch, for example, from necklines to underarm seams. The vice president travels to the plants, sits with the women, listens to them, and gives them encouragement. He also gives them exercises to increase their confidence. And he never lowers the performance requirement. He tells them they are capable and they are to learn the new skill by such and such a date. That is it, no reprieves. His technique is brilliant, and it works. These employees prove capable of what he asks and a lot more. He never gives in to feeling sorry for them, and all of his 700-plus employees make the grade. This man provides support and assistance for these workers without denigrating their potential.

A mature perspective toward helping others challenges them to achieve their full potential.

The World of Achievement

You are on an idyllic vacation in the British Virgin Islands, aboard a chartered yacht, enjoying the fruits of success with your spouse and children, who are delighted and astonished that you are taking the time to snorkel and sail with them. After two days, the yacht's cellular phone rings and calls you back to New York to soothe some important client's ruffled feathers. You surprise your tearful family by having a helicopter pick you up in mid-Caribbean. You are definitely in the world of achievement.

Anyone who works in a 20th-century company knows the pleasure and also the price of achievement. If you do not sell yourself constantly, you will not see yourself come to fruition, at least in this world.

Some people are naturals at packaging and marketing themselves effectively. Jim, a vice president of a Fortune 50 company, has this amazing ability. He always positions himself as a hero and rises quickly to a critical position with the company. His staff calls him *The I-Guy* and you can guess the origin of his nickname. When credit is given, he accepts it as a single-handed achievement, not as a manager with a team of dedicated and gifted professionals behind him.

In a moment of insight and growth, Jim sees that his efforts are focused on himself and bear no relationship to what is best for the company. In business school he was taught to gear every question and remark to subtly enhance himself by downplaying what others said. He begins to rethink his behavior and treatment of the people who work for him. Borrowing ideas from the world of mentoring, he is now concerned to empower others to work effectively, and he ensures they get the credit. As a power-sharing executive, his value to the company is greater than ever. Jim is exactly the sort of executive that companies need today. He listens from the perspective of marketing and packaging but is absolutely committed to integrity and honesty.

A mature perspective toward achievement is equally concerned with the achievements and recognition of others.

The World of Drama

You attend a production of Shakespeare's KING LEAR at the Edinburgh International Arts Festival. The lights in the magnificent theater dim and the audience is hushed. On the suddenly floodlit stage appears Lear, in outlandish garb, proclaiming his madness. As the play unfolds, you are vicariously overwhelmed by the emotions of jealousy, hatred, and betrayal but also of nobility, commitment, loyalty, and steadfastness. You leave profoundly entertained and also shaken by the possibility that similar forces and emotions play a significant role in your own workplace and family. You have entered the world of drama.

As a member of the investment-research department, you are seeking a way to promote and advertise a new mutual fund you helped create. Now you have the novel experience of meeting people from the advertising agency who are to produce a television commercial promoting your creation. You expect a business-like video, perhaps starring yourself dressed in a suit and talking about numbers. What you get is a video with a rock-music track and two attractive females breathlessly discussing the virtues of your new fund between serves on the handball court. You have entered the world of drama.

Whether you are wrapped up in an action-packed adventure movie or listening to juicy tidbits about the latest corporate power struggle, theatrics provide a spice to life. Moreover, they are valuable in business. Facility with drama enables a CEO to paint a future that everyone longs to enjoy. Individuals with this perspective experience life as *the thrill of victory and the agony of defeat.* Journalists concerned about selling copy use skills from this world to enhance every story whether it is about a major earthquake or the local dog show.

The president of the teachers' union in a large midwestern city has held that position for almost 30 years. He is a history teacher and has a dramatic and powerful vision for the professionalization of teachers. His ability to articulate the critical role of teachers has galvanized his following and profoundly affected the school system. He is not as proficient at listening for details to ensure that nothing is missed. To complement his strength, his closest assistant is an individual who excels in organization and the fine points of bringing a vision to fruition.

> A mature perspective toward drama gives a faithful rendition of the facts and details.

The World of Analysis

When you attend a management class on inventory control or plan plumbing modifications in your bathroom, you enter the world of analysis. The world of analysis is the world of science and engineering. From this perspective, the core value is to observe and understand reality. Notice how different this is from, for example, the core value of the dramatic perspective, which values the intensity of experience, or from the perspective of mentoring, which values helping. In 20th-century organizations, analytical skills are highly prized. People comfortable with analysis are likely to enjoy learning throughout their careers. The next step for those who love to analyze is, *Just do it!* Apply your valuable knowledge to the problems you see in your company and community.

In spite of continual enticements, one technical advisor successfully avoids the management trap for many years. He is adamant that he does not wish to be responsible for anyone other than himself. He leaves one company that forces him into a management role and finds an employer with a technical career path. This works out well for him and for his company. He gains wide respect inside the technical organization for his ability to single-handedly invent and implement specialty software for the computer. The day comes when he can see enormous possibilities for a comprehensive automation system to eliminate the overwhelming volume of detail for the computer operators. However, it is far too large a project for him to take on alone. Again he is faced with the prospect of navigating the management channels, gaining the support to undertake the project, and overseeing the work of other technicians. He knows that there is no one other than himself who has the knowledge and understanding to be able to pull the project off successfully. This time he chooses to face the challenge by providing the technical leadership necessary to bring his dream to fruition.

A mature perspective toward analysis does not analyze for its own sake but uses understanding to invent and lead.

The World of Criticism

You watch an action movie that you think is great. Muscled men and women, glistening with seductive sweat, fire ferocious weapons at each other. You have never seen such amazing special effects. Next day you read reviews of the movie in the newspapers. One dismisses it as banal and puerile while another reviewer has the insight to share your opinion. You have entered the world of criticism.

You present your business plan to a group of entrepreneurial coaches. Your business plan is your life, and you have put your heart and soul into it. You are afire with the promise of your invention. Your coaches point out significant, possibly fatal flaws. You are crestfallen. You have entered the world of criticism.

In this world, the core value is surfacing and identifying problems. This focus is a form of academic critique, an examination of the pros and cons. The true champion of debate has no desire to prove others wrong or to be destructive but wishes to act as a devil's advocate and enable the best possible choice of actions.

Two co-workers get into trouble because they live in different worlds. Sue, who tries to make constructive suggestions, antagonizes Ophelia, whose core outlook is dramatic. To Ophelia, the well-intentioned criticisms translate as cynical undermining. Then she learns a simple translation technique for Sue's assessments: *It sounds like heartless criticism, but I know Sue is actually trying to help me.* This mental translation lets her put the criticism to good use rather than being disheartened by it. Similarly, Sue is learning patience with Ophelia's dramatic accounts of everyday events and even discovering the value of praising Ophelia's work before suggesting improvements.

Always the time comes when the power of debate is used to best advantage by setting a positive goal. For example, the materials manager in a processing and packaging plant is approached by employees about racism within the department. Personnel sees a need for diversity training and asks the materials manager to address the problem. The manager meets with the interested employees and together they brainstorm numerous ideas. Then the group seems to become bogged down, debating the same ideas over and over. Solutions are proposed by one or more individuals, then rejected by the others. The manager realizes his group is heavily weighted with critics who can spend hours discussing pros and cons. So he goes into the next meeting and sets a course of action. He asks them to buy into the idea. Commit and just do it. They seem relieved to follow his direction. Over the next several months he reminds them not to second guess themselves but, to follow their chosen course without wavering. They do so, and their program gets off the ground.

A mature perspective toward criticism moves on to make a powerful commitment to a course of action.

The World of New Ideas

You open the latest issue of FORTUNE, and the cover story is about executive dress. You have conservative ideas about how people should dress, perhaps favoring pinstripe double-breasted suits for men and similar outfits for women, except that their shirts can be blouses and have modest pleats or ruffles. What you see on the FORTUNE cover jolts and astonishes you: a costume for a female CEO that looks like Harley Davidson motorcycle garb. You have entered the world of latest fashion.

You work in the design department of Cross. For years you have designed and manufactured slim, elegant pens of silver and gold, that have been the badges of successful and aspiring consultants and executives for decades. One day, almost out of nowhere, Mont Blanc's fat, oversized pens attract the interest of the early adopters of new fashion. Somehow, before long, your elegant, slim pens are passé and sales are in the tank. In response you switch to a line of fat pens. You have entered the fast-changing world of designer products.

When you throw yourself into a wild and powerful brainstorming session, you enter the world of new ideas. This world can be zany and fun. Marketing organizations often create environments to encourage this thinking in their employees. Such environments are a riot of unusual gadgets, toys, unexpected sounds and colors, all designed to stimulate thinking to generate new ideas. This world is especially valuable and not everyone is experienced with it. In many groups, brainstorming sessions flounder, with people stumbling about and never jumping in with both feet. The perspectives of analysis, debate, and even perfection must be left at the door for people to participate energetically in off-the-cuff thinking. Conversely, to be convinced that the latest fad will solve your problems leads to *flavor-of-the-month* programs that race through corporations with the speed of prairie fires.

Many companies experience the effects of separation between their marketing and production departments. Marketing comes up with bold new ideas, complete with a sample, and throws them over the wall to operations. Operations is responsible for figuring how to actually produce a consistent product in volume. Meanwhile, marketing is not waiting at the wall to learn what is happening in production. They have gone on to developing other newer products for next month. One food manufacturing firm encounters this challenge regularly because they compete in the fast changing, advertising-and-fad-dependent arena of children's breakfast food. After a particularly unsuccessful attempt to implement a new product with complex shapes and bright colors, a team leader in the processing department sees the value that can be gained if marketing has a better understanding of what happens to their pilot products in processing. He takes it upon himself to begin a program of interdepartmental cultural exchange with the result that marketing teams begin regularly attending the production design sessions for their new foods.

> A mature perspective toward new ideas is able to focus on one idea and develop it fully.

The World of Power

One of the many attractions of the Colonial Williamsburg restoration is the governor's mansion. You step into a great entrance hall. Immediately your eyes are diverted to the high ceiling where a massive array of shining battle-axes is suspended, arranged in a circle, deadly tips facing toward the center. Your tour guide explains that the intent is to impress the visitor with the power and majesty of the governor, his control of overwhelming force, and the authority vested in him by the king. You have entered the world of power.

Twentieth-century business, at the top levels, is about power. Read between the lines of any issue of THE WALL STREET JOURNAL, BUSINESS WEEK, or FORTUNE. Profits, productivity, and performance are secondary. The true fascination is with power—who has it, who is gaining it, and who is losing it. As you attend business meetings higher and higher in the hierarchy, the underlying preoccupation with the world of power becomes more and more obvious.

> Twentieth-century business is not about profits. It is about power.

Power has two aspects. On one side is the ability to get things done. On the other is the ability to prevent people from getting things done. Power in its positive aspect is immensely valuable and contributes to the welfare of all. Power in its negative aspect is problematic. Saddam Hussein had the power and used it, to lay waste to Kuwait. But he is hated and feared, not admired.

> When you have and use power, it may be useful to ask yourself, from time to time, whether you are using it for positive or negative purposes.

Twentieth-century business tradition emphasizes the decision-making power of top management. As long as the business decisions require the expertise of those at the peak of the hierarchy, all is well. But, in a fast and changing market, it is unlikely that the abilities of the same few people will consistently lead to the best decisions and creativity necessary to thrive in the 21st-century world of business.

The way out is to be open to the contribution of people from different worlds. The world of power needs the contribution of new ideas, analysis, and criticism. For example, the vice president of operations for a mid-size manufacturing firm is unable, initially, to alter the hostile relationship between the union workers and management. Although he sees the futility of the situation, he cannot, from his world view, see what steps will turn the atmosphere around in the plant. The business agent for the union makes several attempts to share his insights with the vice president, to no avail. Then, he offers to buy the vice president a drink. Out of the office setting, the executive is able to hear the business agent's suggestions. The issue hinges on the executive's assumption that it is entirely his personal responsibility to make the plant run well. He looks to no one for support. With the urging of the business agent, he attends several classes on work teams and employee participation. The result is a turnaround in his management style and the beginning of collaborative decision making within the plant.

A mature perspective toward power seeks collaboration and input from diverse perspectives.

The World of Mediation

You are involved in union-management negotiations. The air is heavy and tense with opposed agendas. Sarcastic pleasantries are exchanged before getting down to the business of confrontation. The mediator reminds the participants of their common heritage and purpose. After each acrimonious exchange, the mediator suggests another larger possibility, big enough to include both opposing viewpoints. The union wants job security, and management wants higher profits. The mediator asks whether both interests cannot be served by avoiding a strike and bringing more business to the plant. You have entered the world of mediation.

This world will expand in the 21st-century workplace. As corporations turn to short-term employment and out-sourcing, the possibility of human misunderstanding and miscommunication soars. So do the possibilities for masters of the world of mediation. When you smooth ruffled feathers or encourage collaboration, you are operating with this point of view. People who master this world are peacemakers and often well liked from every side.

The plant manager for a major glass production firm intuitively understands the world of mediation. His skills are greatly appreciated because he can foster cooperation among antagonistic parties. Over the years, his detractors argue that no one in a leadership position should care about peacemaking but should issue orders instead! However, in 21st-century companies, these peacemaking skills are highly prized, and his company offers him a promotion to oversee the company's labor relations with all collective bargaining units. This manager's commitment to the community also leads him to extensive involvement to build partnerships between the city's factions. People begin to ask him whether he would consider entering the political arena.

> A mature perspective toward mediation includes personal expression and achievement.

ACCESSING DIFFERENT WORLDS

By virtue of our perspectives, we live in different worlds. If you communicate using only the conventions of your current or momentary perspective, you will lose, or even alienate, most of your audience. Listen to what people tell you; they are describing the world they see. Ask yourself, again and again, *What would I have to see to make me say that?* This helps you to listen behind the words, to experience the world they perceive. If you cannot figure out the source of the words, then ask. *What do you see that makes you say that?* Or, *Tell me more about that.* You will discover that people are delighted to tell you more. Sometimes you may see their confusion and surprise that you do not already know— because they assume that your world is exactly like theirs!

In a school district, representatives of the tradespeople, the food service staff, the secretaries, the cleaning staff, and the bus drivers are asked what they would like to have happen, more than anything else. Unanimously they respond, *We would like to see everyone respected in the schools.* What causes people to wish for this more than for money or benefits or working conditions? As you might suspect, they do not feel respected. Of course, it would be easy to dismiss what these people have to say. Perhaps they are overly sensitive or too demanding. Yet they are telling the truth, describing the world in which they live. To bridge the gulf to their world and to every world we encounter calls for accepting what we learn without judgment, and responding to the learning. This acceptance allows each conversation to reach its own potential. Conversations in which people genuinely listen and respond are not only gratifying but far more productive than a scripted conversation can ever be.

8

Create Real Results

Whatsoever thy hand findeth to do, do it with all thy might; for there is
no device, nor knowledge, nor wisdom, in the grave, whither thou
goest.

ECCLESIASTES

BEFORE READING THIS CHAPTER:

Make a list for yourself of three problems that you face today due to lack
of money or time, or some other measurable, scarce commodity. For example,

- Do you yearn for an exotic vacation but cannot afford the
  money or the time?
- Are you facing a major project and there absolutely, positively
  is not enough time to get the work done?
- Are you unable to get the job that you want because you do
  not have the credentials?
- Are you unable to retire because you do not have the money?
- Do you consider corporate performance assessments a waste
  since they do not help people change?

Each of these situations is a case where the hard evidence seems an impenetrable barrier to achieving what you want. Write your specific issues down and keep them in front of you as you read. There are questions throughout the chapter pertaining to your issues. Answer the questions and by the time you complete the chapter you may see new action to take to resolve your concerns.

The fact is, people believe in numbers. We believe they represent some real perspective on the universe and provide us with real information about the way the world behaves. If we can gather enough information, enough numbers, then we can figure out what is going on and what action will put us in control of our environment. This chapter challenges this thinking and offers a 21st-century perspective on measurement and metrics, emphasizing the most formidable arena of seemingly hard fact—cold hard cash.

WHAT IS WEALTH?

According to a detailed NEW YORK TIMES account, James is a healthy, 52-year-old man who began as a machinist and worked his way to plant manager.[1] He has equity in an expensive home in California, grown children who are pursuing careers, a wife who works, $300,000 in the bank, and a retirement dream involving water and boats. Is this man wealthy? Well, you may think so and even comment that it sounds as though he could retire now. Another person may observe that, *As long as he has his health he is certainly wealthy*. A third person could point out, *Anyone who works himself up from machinist to plant manager must be intelligent and talented.*

But James does not consider himself wealthy. He was laid off three years ago by Kodak and has not worked since. Back then, James pulled down $130,000 a year in a position representing the culmination of 25 years of loyal and excellent service to his company. But now the plant he managed is closed. Nonetheless, James still dresses in pressed suit and starched shirt, to meet occasionally with his executive-support-group lunch where they advise him to cling to the trappings of his self-image

---

[1]"Big Holes Where Dignity Used to Be," by Rick Bragg, *New York Times*, March 5, 1996, p. 1ff.

and lifestyle. So three years, 2000 resumes, and 10 interviews later he is driving a Mercedes that now needs transmission work, still paying $2000 a month for his mortgage, watching his savings disappear, and bemoaning that he will never realize his dream of retirement in Florida.

What is wealth? In common usage wealth refers to a *large amount of money or personal possessions*. But there is also a second meaning: *an abundance of anything*. Although the tendency is to determine our wealth by counting our money, a 21st-century perspective on wealth suggests the question: *What results are you trying to achieve?*

> True wealth may not be as adequately measured by a bank account balance as by the answer to this: Have you generated an abundance of the results that you want?

Perhaps that is the true measure of your personal wealth. For example, many of us consider Mother Theresa to be wealthy, yet she has nothing in the way of personal possessions or money and has no interest in generating personal wealth. Mother Theresa has devoted her life to caring for the abandoned and dying people of Calcutta. She has inspired others to follow her footsteps and generated an outpouring of love around the world. In the arena of love she has an abundance of results for her efforts.

In measuring personal wealth, the role of money is profoundly misunderstood. For many of us, money has become the primary focus of our lives. It could be that focusing so hard on money undermines other, equally vital, life objectives. And paradoxically, an imprisoning focus on money may actually cost us the achievement of the results we care about producing, including money itself.

According to our country's Declaration of Independence, life, liberty and the pursuit of happiness are basic values. In the 20th century, we seem to have concluded that money is the key to happiness. Yet money and happiness have no relation to each other. One survey asked

1000 people how much they made and how happy they were, on a scale where 1= miserable, 3= can't complain, and 5= joyous.[1] The results show no correlation at all:

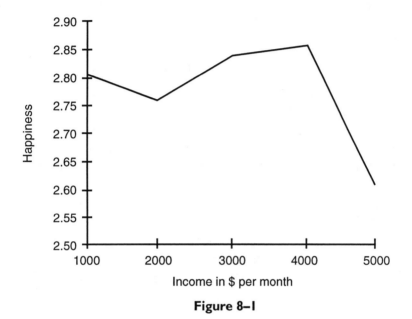

Figure 8–1

A possible mistake in 20th-century thinking may be the assumption that:

Value-of-money = amount-of-money

But what if:

Value-of-money = encompassing-circumstances-factor
<u>TIMES</u> amount-of-money

---

[1]Dominguea and Robin, *Your Money or Your Life*, Penguin Books, 1992.

where the encompassing-circumstances factor can vary from infinitely negative to infinitely positive. The encompassing-circumstances factor is a number that you assign based on whether, and how much, your life is fruitful in whatever is important to you. To set its value you answer questions like these. *What is the quality of your marriage and your relationship with your children? How is your health? Is your work gratifying?* With the new formula there is greater leverage in changing the encompassing circumstances than in changing the amount of money, if what you want from money is value.

We assign to our money a fixed value, because we measure it in numerical terms. One hundred thousand dollars appears to have a set value. But it is not so. The value is continually fluctuating, an infinitely complex function of the encompassing circumstances in which we find ourselves at any moment.

To millionaire Paul, $100,000 is the loose change lost in the unpredictable variations of the Arizona real-estate market in the particular month he decides to change his life and sell his home. To Tom and Judy, whose daughter is terminally ill, $100,000 is irrelevant because money will not make her well again. To Ron and Jenny, $100,000 is a deluxe world cruise, the reward of a lifetime of hard work, and unexpectedly given to them by loving children. To Eustace and Mabel, $100,000 is independent wealth, financing all they will ever need to enjoy their unconventionally luxurious villa with no utilities, but three servants, on the majestic Mexican Pacific coast.

> The value of money is not fixed at all, but varies profoundly depending on who has it and what their circumstances are.

Think about money you have spent over the years. Was not some ill spent and some well spent? Do you have, for example, a prize possession or experience—perhaps a piece of furniture, a tool, a course you took, a blow-out vacation, or even a gift you gave—that has returned immense value to you? Our friend Don Feinberg is clear on the best money he has ever spent:

The return-on-investment from owning a dishwasher is damn near infinite.

As you can tell, Don's encompassing-circumstances factor is quite high for his dishwasher dollars. On the other hand, is there money you have spent that has been totally wasted or has even caused you misery? Holly spends $250.00 for a garden sundial from an attractive catalog. She never gets around to putting it in the garden and ultimately sells it in a yard sale 10 years later for $2.00. Jack takes his parents out for a gourmet dinner at an exclusive restaurant. The waiters are haughty, the food is mediocre, and his parents, used to informality at home, are miserable. Paul spends $40,000 to purchase the sports car of his dreams. The vehicle requires constant service and is in the repair shop almost as frequently as on the road.

THE MEANING OF METRICS

Objective measurement is the byword of corporate thinking today. Tighten up the numbers, show the real results. Managers believe performance appraisals and skill assessment programs characterize and quantify people. This thinking is a consequence of 20th-century perspective. The whole idea of measurement is to objectify or remove human qualities and concerns from the matter.

Twenty-first-century thinking asserts the radical view that all assessment is misleading and that the act of assessment itself strips human meaning from whatever is being measured.

Because of our 20th-century perspective on our personal wealth and corporate profits, we are fooled continually into thinking that whatever we care about can be quantified and measured and that the results generated from this perspective have meaning.

> Only rarely is there value in compiling facts and figures.

We think we need facts to orient ourselves, to get our bearings, perhaps to select a course of action. In other words, we use facts to discover what the world is like. But this implies that there is an objective world to discover. What if there is not? What if we are actually using the so-called facts to create the world for ourselves? For example, there is a great deal of doomsaying today on the economy. A much-touted statistic to prove that the working masses are downtrodden is that more than 43 million jobs have been erased in the United States since 1979. A competing statistic is that, in this same period, 70 million jobs were created. Suppose you are a modern day Rip Van Winkle, asleep since 1979, and when you awake these are the only two pieces of information you know about the state of the country today. What would you extrapolate and use to form your new image of the nation? Would you immediately assume the economy is up? Or would you focus on the millions who have been displaced? Would you fear that they are still unemployed and suffering? Would you demand to know what the government is doing about the turmoil? Would you simply be interested to learn about what the new jobs are? In other words, using just these two numbers, you have the freedom to create the world as you choose. It is not that one of these numbers is right and the other is wrong.

> The meaning of any metric is created entirely through human interpretation.

Twentieth-century thinking is mesmerized by numbers, continually confusing them with context. This is what occurs when political views polarize. Both sides shout numbers and statistics at one another, each thinking that their numbers and statistics settle the matter clearly in their favor. But the numbers settle nothing at all. It is the perspective of the people who are listening that carries the day. If you have lost your job when it was moved overseas and a politician talks about *closing the borders and circling the wagons* it might sound like a good idea. If you are well paid and see 36 percent of your income go to the government each year, a flat-tax politician may be appealing.

Perhaps it appears to you that measurement at least provides valuable information to choose what to do. But is it really so? Or is it possible we first select a course of action that matches our world view and then search out the supporting numbers?

TWELVE STEPS TO THE TOP LINE

The following twelve sections give specific tools to create results where money, time, assessments and measurements of all kind are concerned. Readers familiar with THE PHOENIX AGENDA will recognize that these steps are a modification of that book's twelve facets, applied to the context of wealth creation. To get the most benefit from what follows, answer the questions at the end of each section keeping in mind the issues you identified for yourself at the beginning of the chapter.

Begin with Trust

Trust is the bedrock of all human affairs.

> Where there is trust, the numbers do not matter. Equally, where there is no trust, the numbers do not matter.

For example, a smart materials-handling manager hears from corporate that his loading dock is responsible for high product-damage rates. He knows the bad reputation of his department is undeserved but cannot prove it because there is no damage-tracking process to gather that information. Instead, he invites the corporate quality team to meet with his line organization to discuss how to improve quality. As an immediate result, the damage reports decrease, and the reputation of his department improves dramatically. The meeting has convinced both groups they want to achieve the same results and has empowered them to work together rather than take potshots at one another. Later, when a quality tracking system is installed it serves to further the positive momentum between the two groups.

The most fundamental trust that any of us can have is in ourselves, our worth, and our ability. One married couple, on reaching their mid-forties, realize that a dream they share is paying off their mortgage as quickly as possible. They talk to a financial advisor about this and he strongly discourages them from doing so. *Paying off your mortgage is an unwise investment*, he tells them. *Put your money in the stock market where you will get a better return.* They take his advice but continue to talk about the freedom they would feel if they did not have that monthly payment. Ultimately they choose to trust their own judgment and begin putting extra money toward their mortgage. The next time they meet with the financial advisor he admits, *Among the retired people I know, the happiest are those who have paid off their mortgage.*

Trust yourself to know what return-on-investment is best for you.

- ◆ Where would greater trust help resolve the issues you face?
- ◆ How can you put trust in place?
- ◆ Will it make a difference if you give trust as a gift? If so, will you do that?

Uncover Concerns

When people have different perspectives, they may interpret specific measures differently. Even when people want exactly the same result, their ideas about how to achieve the result may sound alien to one another. Consider this example. A manager writes five numbers on the board—the cost of production for his own plant and four others. The number for his plant is the second highest. *Where do you suppose the business will go?* he asks. *We simply have no choice but to cut costs!* The head of the union turns red with anger and exclaims, *I don't give a damn about cost! I want to be sure my people all have jobs and the plant doesn't shut down the way that Buffalo did!* Can you see that the union leader and the department manager want exactly the same thing? Both are absolutely committed to the future of the plant. Nonetheless their starting points to achieve the goal are miles apart. The manager focuses on the cost factor, which determines whether headquarters allocates more or less production to the plant. The union leader has an unspoken concern that cost cutting means job loss and that the manager may even have a hidden agenda to lay people off. The tension can dissolve if the manager acknowledges the union leader's concern and indicates that he, too, wants to see everyone remain employed.

Numbers do not win arguments. To work effectively with people you must listen and speak to their underlying concerns.

♦ Relative to your issues, what are the unspoken or background concerns of other people? What are your own worst fears?
♦ What action can you take to validate or address these concerns? Will you do that?

Speak the Future—Do It Now

Assessments and judgments are based on past events. It is not possible to assess what has not yet happened. Even projections based on previous experience are guesses about the future. Twentieth-century speaking relies heavily on analysis and evaluation, the purpose of which is to try to predict the events of tomorrow. Twenty-first-century thinking proposes that the future is created by what you say. What you have to say this very minute creates the world we will live in tomorrow. As you can see, in the 21st-century world, assessments and judgments are lethal weapons. Assessments and judgments have the power to kill new possibilities for the future, ordaining instead a future that merely replays the past.

In business, pay and promotions are often based on written evaluations of past work, called performance appraisals. Most such assessments recount the so-called facts about an individual's past performance to enable better performance for the future. Too often the effect is exactly reversed. An assessment points out faults and flaws which can actually trap the person into the same old behaviors. Other than sending the person off to training seminars, management knows little about enabling the individual to develop new skills. One manager learns a great deal about changing behavior when she puts aside the corporate appraisal forms. Instead she begins by making a list of her vision and commitments for the employee. The list is not intended to be a reflection of the past or a list of capabilities the person already exhibits. Rather, she makes it up to reflect the growth and development she believes will be the most powerful for the employee. For example,

> *I am committed to Sam's capability as a great manager and I know he can do it.*

> *I am committed to Sam's ability to speak to the members of his staff with sensitivity and I already see evidence of that.*

> *I am committed to Sam's ability to provide just the right amount of technical guidance for his staff and I see him doing that now.*

As she said, *None of this is true. I simply write and design a pair of powerful shoes for the person to step into. What is most fascinating to me is that once I have done this, I can always find evidence that the most outrageous changes are already in progress. I make sure those bits of evidence go onto the appraisal form. Almost always the person is greatly empowered to make a habit of the effective behaviors and experiment with other new skills.*

> The future has not happened yet. Our most powerful tool for creating it is what we say.

- ◆ If your issue(s) is resolved, how will the resolution make the future brighter?
- ◆ Who can help you resolve your issue(s)? How will the new future benefit them?
- ◆ Have you spoken to them about these benefits? If not, will you do that?

Set Strategies to Form the Future

To realize your vision it is valuable to lay out interim accomplishments. These are the strategies or goals to bridge the gap between the present situation and the reality you choose for your future. Strategies support bringing the future into being and, as such, they are part of the creation process. Strategies also make it possible to identify appropriate actions to fulfill your dreams.

Nonetheless, strategies are not visions. Strategies support or serve visions. Setting a strategy is much like naming something. Naming focuses your energy but can blind you to everything else. Only the vision gives inspiration and without that, strategies are lifeless and irrelevant. Have you ever felt you are just slogging it out? If so, the chances are high that you have lost sight of the inspiration behind your objective.

> Goals that can be measured have been stripped of human meaning.

The true value to achieving your goals always and only lies in the human initiative that gives rise to them.

For example, suppose you run a computer products firm and your vision is to provide premier equipment to your customers. *Perfect Products* is your motto, and you become known in the industry for exactly that. Your most important goal is absolutely, positively, no flaws, ever, in the equipment you sell. All goes well until one day when a customer calls to report a problem with one of your computers. You insist it cannot be true. Then, another call and another error. Suddenly there are dozens of calls flooding your customer service phone lines. In a replay of your most hideous nightmare, the vice president of Product Development rushes in to inform you that the worst is true, the product is flawed. By this time the news media has heard about your troubles, and reporters are lining up at your door for a public statement. What now? Do you insist that your products are faultless? To admit the errors is a clear failure to meet your most important goal. To hide your failure, however, could be a grave violation of the heart in your company vision.

With these admonitions in mind, what follows is a simple, powerful two-step procedure. These steps can help high-powered corporate groups devise strategic plans, as well as support individuals to map out life and career goals. The extreme simplicity and flexibility of the tools are part of their appeal.

The idea is to break any complex goal or project down into no more than five critical factors or attributes: the five major things that must happen in order for you to achieve your objective. You name each goal, assign it a measure, and then map out worst-case, planned-levels, and best-case measures.

Here is an example, filled in by a business consultant engaged in business planning for himself. First he states a vision.

> *The vision of this project is to reach people who are committed to fulfillment in work for themselves and others, people who will use contextual thinking wisely and well to improve their own lives and the lives of everyone they meet.*

Identifying Multiple Goals

	Goals	Measures	Worst Case	Planned Level	Best Case
1	Publish book	Books sold	5000	50000	100000
2	Consulting	New customers	1	3	5
3	Create audio tapes	Tapes sold	10	100	1000
4	Public speaking	# of speeches	1	5	12

Figure 8–2

Notice that the tool asks for worst, planned and best levels of the measures. The worst level for each goal is a level below which the achievement of the goal is considered a failure. Conversely, the tool also asks for best-case levels. This step is crucial—you select a best case as that level beyond which you will devote no more energy to that particular goal. Without the best-and-worst-case scenarios, the pursuit of goals can spin out of control and become addictive. While you might think that no limit is a better idea, a goal without limit could require the investment of resources without limit, and could lead to burnout and neglect of other priorities.

Situations of human interest are complex with many interwoven events and possible strategies to influence future events. But our education and training, even verbal communication—which presents ideas one at a time—limit our ability to think about interacting and multiple ideas concurrently. This tool helps set multiple simultaneous goals.

Any group, be they a product-development team or a Fortune 500 executive committee, can do this simple exercise of multiple goal setting. Limiting the number of top goals to 5 produces focus. Setting simple measures gives everyone extreme clarity about what is to be achieved. And setting worst, planned, and best levels of the success measures keeps the overall project and its components on track. Finally the tool is so simple and quick to use that new attributes and levels can be created whenever necessary.

The following section, TAKE ACTION TO SUPPORT YOUR STRATEGIES shows how to develop and evaluate action plans in terms of their ability to achieve not just one but the entire set of goals simultaneously. Before looking ahead, though, you might want to fill out a goals table for yourself. Remember to state your project vision.

Identifying Multiple Goals

	Goals	Measures	Worst Case	Planned Level	Best Case
1					
2					
3					
4					
5					

Figure 8–3

Take Action to Support Your Strategies

In the previous section SET STRATEGIES TO FORM THE FUTURE, a simple yet powerful method for listing business or personal goals and quantifying measures of success is described. Here is the companion tool—for selecting a course of action sufficient to achieve all of your goals.

Here you can see some of the actions selected by the consultant and his estimation of their impact on the achievement of his goals.

To use this tool, first brainstorm various methods or action plans that appear to be related to your goals. Then fill in the table to see how all of your planned actions affect all of your goals. If you feel that one method alone will assure that you reach the goal, assign it a value of 100 percent. If a method makes a substantial contribution, assign it 50 percent. For a marginal contribution, use 5 percent.

These are simple, effective tools. They use numbers, not to describe the past, but to map out a desired future. They can be used by a diverse group representing all levels of the company, including customers and suppliers. The tools appeal to analytical minds and yet provide a simple systems perspective (by looking at a complete set of goals). Try filling in the following table for your project.

Estimating Impact of Actions on Goals

GOALS	Get book reviews in 10 business publications	Ask current customers for referrals	Create audio tapes to supplement key chapters	Call contacts for 6 business organizations	Total Impact for each goal
Publish book	100%	0%	5%	5%	110%
Consulting	5%	100%	0%	5%	110%
Create audio tapes	5%	5%	100%	5%	115%
Public speaking	5%	50%	5%	50%	110%
Total Impact for each action	115%	155%	110%	65%	

(ACTIONS across top)

Figure 8–4

Estimating Impact of Actions on Goals

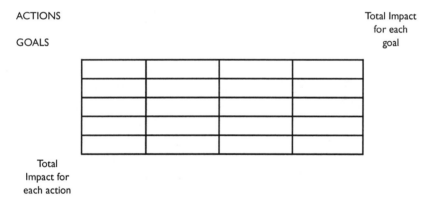

ACTIONS

GOALS

Total Impact for each goal

Total Impact for each action

Figure 8–5

Profit from Problems

James, the plant manager (described earlier in this chapter) who was laid off when the plant was shut down, is experiencing a moment of truth. Unemployed, with loss of a paycheck, his carefully laid plans for his future have gone up in smoke. Currently, he is experiencing depression and paralysis, a common reaction to such an event.

There is, however, a constructive way to use upsets to further our plans. If there are no problems, no blockades suddenly arising to disrupt our well-laid plans, there is no need for innovation. Problems are a source of new thinking, of new possibilities. It may be that problems are the only source of new ideas and significant progress. This is not a new claim—the philosophy and ancient common wisdom from many cultures contains the same idea. The Chinese character for *crisis* also means *opportunity*.

In just such an example, the supervisors at one factory are told they are no longer eligible for overtime pay. For several of them this policy change cuts their income by as much as 25%. Yet, a few months later they are unanimously pleased with the change and have no interest in returning to the old system. All have discovered excellent uses for their new-found free time. The work load is still heavy but now they do not feel guilty going home at quitting time. There is no longer the dilemma of earning money for the family vs. spending time with the family. A few have chosen to return to school and finish a college degree. Others have started a sideline business. The supervisors use the crisis as an opportunity to re-examine their life goals and search out appropriate new courses of action.

To turn any crisis into an opportunity, ask a councilor or trusted friend to ask you these five questions. Stick with each question until your friend fully understands your answers and is satisfied that you will take the action you set for yourself.

- ♦ What is the crisis?
- ♦ What is your basic mission, purpose, or goal that this crisis interrupts?
- ♦ What new courses of action are now possible, especially ones that were unthinkable or impossible before the crisis?
- ♦ Who or what can help?
- ♦ What action are you willing to take now? By when will you take it?

When you engage in such a dialog, you are almost certain to discover new courses of action you could not think of before. You may find that you become an expert at finding new opportunities. Instead of dreading crises, you may start creating them deliberately to experience the benefits.

Use Awareness to Build Momentum

Awareness refers to being conscious of something, holding it in the forefront of your attention. What gets your attention is more likely to get done. Often a simple Post-It is sufficient for a reminder. But visible, creative, compelling, and innovative displays have a surprising power to propel and focus an entire group of people. Who will ever forget *The Economy, Stupid* sign that galvanized and focused Bill Clinton's successful 1992 presidential campaign?

An example of using awareness to boost profits occurs for a team of technicians when they face a schedule requiring them to accomplish more than 60 weeks of work in 30 weeks of time. With traditional scheduling, there is simply no way the work can be completed. As if to defy the constraints of time, they identify all of the tasks and set up a library system to allow each person to choose his or her own task and sign it out of the library. The completed task is returned and another selection made. The *coup de grace* is the large poster they erect in the center of their work area. The poster shows all of the project tasks. As each is finished it is removed from the incomplete task list and added to a pictorial scale for completed work. Every member of the team remains constantly aware of their total progress. As the days pass the excitement and momentum build. Ultimately they accomplish 56 weeks of work in 30 weeks. What remains are non-critical tasks. The team members accomplished this outrageous goal by throwing out the evidence that it could not be done, focusing instead on the evidence of their daily achievements.

- ♦ What task or activity that would contribute to the resolution of your issue(s), never seems to get done, or never gets done right?
- ♦ What display or other memory system could you set up to remind you of the task or of the right way to do it?
- ♦ What work are you facing that absolutely cannot be completed in the allotted time?

- In what way could you throw out the traditional system that reinforces the idea that it cannot be done?
- What new system could you design to focus on your achievement as it happens?

Appreciate Your Wealth

Is winning the only thing? And what constitutes winning? By measuring results we recognize the winners. But are we giving short shrift to the losers? Is it possible that the loser's contribution is as important as that of the winner? In the matter of government, for example, the democratic process cannot exist without a losing candidate. The *also-ran* upholds electoral freedom. The opposition candidate often has a crucial impact on the political conversation. The polls for the 1992 Presidential election showed that Ross Perot had absolutely no chance of winning. Yet the issues he raised regarding fiscal policy, a balanced budget, and even the possibility of a third party have had a substantial impact on subsequent political events. Focusing exclusively on who gets the promotion and title or reading only the books on the NEW YORK TIMES bestseller list may blind us to the variety of our own and others' accomplishments.

In the mid-1980s a few brilliant engineers at Xerox Corporation develop a graphical interface for computers. The Xerox Star uses pictures (called icons), a pointer (called a mouse), and numerous other innovations all for the purpose of making computers user friendly. But the Star is a flat-out commercial failure. The graphical interface concept is so revolutionary that no one knows what to make of it. Yet before it disappears, two engineers become personally intrigued with the idea. Soon they start their own company, called Apple Computer, and use the graphical interface to create a home-computer revolution. Anyone can learn to use these new home computers and thousands of people do. The ideas are then picked up by another young company, Microsoft, and used to design a graphical interface for the IBM personal computer. This touches off a war between Apple and Microsoft as they compete for buyers. Eventually, Apple's profits decline. Is it a failure for Xerox that they invented the graphical interface but did not make a financial success of it? Is Apple a failure because, after a decade at the peak of the industry, they topple? When will we know whether Microsoft Windows is a permanent success? Xerox created a new world of communication, entertainment, and education and affected the course of history when they invented graphical interface. Apple developed the dream and turned it into reality. If we attempt to assess some final score to determine the winners and the losers, then no one is ever a winner. Sooner or later, every product, every person, every company will die.

If wealth is an *abundance or profusion of anything* what do you have in rich profusion that constitutes your wealth?

+ What goals have you undertaken where you felt the outcome was a failure, or at least not what you wanted?
+ List at least three hidden accomplishments that resulted specifically because of the failure to reach your initial goal.
+ Do you now still see the outcome as a failure?

Plant Seeds for Future Wealth

What seeds are you sowing in business? Or with your finances? What are you expecting to reap? By looking into what you want for the future, you will see clearly what kind of action to take today. For example, a woman, just moved to Arizona, finds herself in the searing sun of the parking lot for the Department of Motor Vehicles. She has just found out she must hand in her old plates and is wondering how she will manage to do that with no tools other than her bare hands. A man approaches her carrying a screwdriver and a pliers. *Hello. My name is Bob Vollman, can I help?* He quickly removes the plates and hands them to her. She is astonished. Why would he do this? What does he want? She thanks him as he hands her his business card. *I sell auto insurance. If you would like me to give you a quote, please call.* With that he disappears into the afternoon sun. The woman is so amazed she calls him the next day. *As you might guess, Bob wrote the car insurance, not to mention the home, life, health and business insurance as well.* The afternoon this man spends in the blazing sun is not a guarantee of future business. Yet, the very nature of his action (helping people) expresses a personal perspective on service that makes an impression on the people he assists.

- ◆ What future results would you like to produce that you have not yet been able to produce?
- ◆ What action can you take today that will enable the results you want?
- ◆ When will you take that action?

Create Freedom for Yourself

I couldn't sleep. I would wake up worrying over whether to buy or to sell. I would become extremely distraught and depressed when one of my stocks dropped in value. It was completely out of proportion to the money involved, but I couldn't seem to strike a balance in my behavior. I was addicted, and the only solution was to quit cold turkey. These are the reflective words of a man who began trading a few stocks just to learn about the market. He read many books before making any investment. Soon he spent his evenings downloading the day's market prices onto his home computer and poring over the information. He stopped eating dinner with the family because it took too much time away from planning his buying and selling for the next day. This routine continued for several months until, on a single day, he sold his stocks and stopped playing the market. He adds, *That was a few years ago and I still get queasy when I see that one of my old stocks has shot up or plummeted out of sight.*

As this man saw, the key is freedom. In any activity where there is no freedom to change behavior or do something different, an addiction is at play. Money, especially, is a narcotic although it is rarely recognized as addictive. Perhaps this is because money addictions, although sometimes the source of crime, are often the root of socially acceptable behaviors such as compulsions to work or the drive to succeed.

Addictions to money can include more than just the need to make or spend money. Rob and Joan pride themselves on *not* spending their hard earned dollars. They look down on their friends and family who seem to be constantly shopping, and refuse to get sucked into such rampant consumerism. They buy only used clothes, live in a small home in an unprepossessing neighborhood, and drive a battered green Pinto with almost 200,000 miles on the odometer. On a hot, sunny afternoon, with their baby daughter in the back seat, Joan leaves the grocery store and heads for home. But this time, when she cranks the engine, flames shoot out from under the hood. She jumps out of the car and pulls at the driver's seat to reach her daughter in back. But the driver's seat is jammed. She grabs the seat and yanks harder, and still the seat does not give. Frantic, she races around the car, throws open the passenger door and snatches her daughter to safety. The next day, these grateful parents purchase an expensive new minivan. *All I could think about later was what if our daughter had been burned or killed because we were too cheap to buy a good car. It's not as though we couldn't afford it. I learned an awful lot about money that day.*

Is there anything you always must have, must buy, must eat, or must give? Is there anything you cannot ever have, cannot ever buy, cannot ever eat, or cannot ever give? If so, altering that behavior can be the source of new freedom and enjoyment in your life.

- ♦ In what area of your behavior with money, time, or any activity, are you unable to easily alter your behavior?
- ♦ What freedom would you like to display in that arena?
- ♦ What step can you take? When will you do that?

Mark the Past Paid in Full

James, the unemployed plant manager, is unable to let go of the past. He daily attends an executive support group which encourages him to retain the suit-and-silk-tie trappings of his former existence. This resoluteness may, inadvertently, prevent him from seeing the limitless possibilities of futures that are completely unlike his past. James cannot get on with building a new life because he has not put the old to rest.

Status and position are difficult to relinquish. Money can also haunt us long after it is gone. Have you ever berated yourself, over and over, for money unwisely spent? One woman with an annual salary over six figures gets upset every time she throws away food. *I feel I've wasted money*, she says. Then she discovers a simple ritual that solves her problem. *I figure out how much the food is worth, perhaps a few dollars, and remind myself that if this is the only money I ever squander then I am managing my money pretty well. Every week I put the old food down the garbage disposal along with my judgments about waste.*

For another man who sees the need to let go, the amount is a half-million dollars. As part owner and sole operator of a cable television company, Bob's employment agreement is airtight. Yet the company chooses not to pay him when he is laid off. After a year of fruitless negotiating, Bob files a law suit. He tells the attorney, *The matter is in your hands now. I have to get on with my life. I refuse to be stuck in the past for the sake of money.* Whether the amount can be measured in pennies or fortunes, the need to close the past in order to *get on with life* is the same.

One woman says she has learned more about money from a conversation with her husband than from all of her other experiences combined. Whenever she is concerned that they have spent too much, he says, *Let it go. If we spend every dime we have, there's more where that came from. The money we have was earned through our integrity, industry and ability. Those qualities are our wealth. We can always earn more money.* This man knows the true source of money and it has brought him peace of mind.

- ♦ In what ways do you continue to relive the past with regard to earnings, investments or expenditures?
- ♦ What measurements, such as past failures in school, your age, or your I.Q., are a continuing source of incompletion for you?
- ♦ What ritual can you make up to put the matter to rest once and for all?

Give with Gratitude

In the words of Andrew Carnegie, *The man who dies rich, dies disgraced.* Yet all of us always have something to give, although it may not be measured in dollars. Indeed, it is this willingness or unwillingness to give that creates the fabric of the world around us. Most people have stories such as the following to tell. Their beauty lies in the gift that is given without the expectation or desire to receive anything in return.

There I was, just arrived in the Des Moines airport, with 120 miles to drive to my destination. And I had forgotten my driver's license. All I had was a single credit card. What was I to do? With no idea of what will happen, this woman explains her problem to the clerk at the National Car rental counter. Just then the manager walks out of the office and the clerk tells him the problem. The manager glances briefly at this person who has the audacity to want a car without showing a valid driver's license. He looks back to the clerk and says quietly, *Give her the car*, and walks away. *I couldn't believe it. I've never been back to Des Moines and I don't even know his name. I was so shocked I'm not sure I said thanks.*

Even more amazing is this story of many people, in unison, giving their best performance, with no return for themselves. Rohr Industries announces the closing of their Auburn, Washington, plant in May 1992. The plant continues to operate until the end of November that year. At the time of the closing announcement, Auburn already leads the company in every measurement for product quality. Yet, from May through November, quality continues to improve. Schedule reliability remains at 100%, work transfers from the IAM union workers to nonunion plants are achieved ahead of schedule. There is no loss of equipment or any vandalism. The order of layoffs is determined by union and management, without regard for seniority. In the words of the plant manager, Ernie Bailey, *Our people picked up on the idea of Finishing With Pride and at every level, the people we needed stayed on voluntarily.* These workers gave their top level performance, for no reason, with no hope of reward, because they chose to do so.

Why would anyone make this choice? Facing unemployment does not seem like a time to be grateful. Yet if we choose, there is always the possibility of gratitude. And the giving that results naturally from gratitude may be a major source of joy and happiness in our lives.

- ◆ Where do you already give with gratitude?
- ◆ Where else would you like to give? When will you do that?

9

Dissolve Any Dispute

The thing of it is, a guy's close to ya, ya can't slight 'im. Ya can't slight that guy. A real grievance can be resolved. Differences can be resolved. But an imaginary hurt, a slight, that guy's gonna hate you 'til the day he dies.

JACK NICHOLSON AS JAMES R. HOFFA IN THE 1992 MOVIE "HOFFA"

STRIFE TRANSFORMED

One possibility of 21st-century thinking is that people could get along more productively with one another at home and at work. Whether you wish to succeed in marriage, your own business, a mega-corporation, or whether you simply want to end each day with accomplishment and serenity, the skill of transforming the energy of disputes into a force for focused collaboration can make your wish happen. The 50 percent divorce rate today is evidence of our woeful inability to create peace and joy even in our homes where we most long to do so. And as the world in which we move grows increasingly divergent, the subtle skill of finding common ground among people of varied cultures and experience is critical to the well-being of our communities. This chapter shows how quarrels, disagreements, and simple failures to communicate are always a consequence of mismatched personal perspectives, and teaches a method for dissolving even the worst disputes. Furthermore, where there is anger, there is energy. Energy that today is spent in stubborn bitter battles can actually be harnessed for remarkable achievements.

I don't want the people who work for me to get along! They SHOULD be duking it out for resources! That's how I can tell who deserves the promotion. These are the words of a manager locked in a 20th-century perspective. What corporate worker has not reported to someone who at least rewarded the winners, if not openly encouraged the war? In the corporate jungle, survival of the fittest is exploited to determine who is most likely to bring in big profits for the company. A vice president for one mega-corporation likens the executive environment to a game of jai-alai where the players are forever pitted against one another. The reward for winning is that you gain status and are allowed to continue playing. To play is to face constant challenges from newcomers whose acquired stature is not so great as yours. But if you are even once beaten, you fall from your elevated position to that of a beginning player. Although real-life players in the corporate arena grow frustrated and exhausted with the wastefulness of the game, there is no shortage of up-and-coming professionals happy to replace them when they tire or make a false move.

Is this really the most productive approach to business? A midwestern manufacturing plant has a 40-year history of struggle and strife between management and union. Sometimes management wins and sometimes the union holds the trump. The upper hand goes back and forth between the antagonists. If it ever worked well, such a system no longer works. The cost in productivity causes this plant to plummet to the bottom of the corporate rating system. The future holds only the promise of an eventual shutdown if nothing is done to intervene. The situation is turned around by a 21st-century manager committed to collaboration, respect, and teamwork. Within a year the plant goes from one of the least, to the most productive in the corporate system. Today, the manager chuckles and remembers that, according to old corporate-performance appraisals, he spends too time peacemaking when he should instead be issuing orders.

Is conflict inevitable? From the 20th-century perspective all goods are in short supply, and people are pitted against one another to acquire what they need and want. Thus, conflict cannot be avoided. For the protagonists in a midwestern public school system, the conflict revolves around the question: *Who is in charge?* as though the amount of available authority is limited. Who is best suited to set the curriculum or select the textbooks? Who controls the classroom? What is the role of the principal? Who should evaluate the teachers?

> **From a 21st-century perspective all disputes are only apparent. They are the result of people using different perspectives.**

When these perspectives collide, it can appear to each person that the other parties are behaving foolishly, dishonestly, or unreliably. A young couple almost comes to a parting of the ways because neither is willing to be the first to commit. He is remodeling his house and expects her to pitch in and help. His first wife walked out suddenly after several years, and he wants his friend to prove she is committed to their relationship. His friend, however, was taken advantage of in earlier relationships and is afraid he could be doing the same. She offers to work with him on the weekends for pay. He is offended and angry. History leads both of them to measure carefully how much they contribute of themselves to the relationship.

> **Disagreements are never about the issue at hand. They are always rooted in the interpretation of past events as hurts and slights.**

With encouragement from friends, this couple converses in depth about past experiences that formed their present viewpoints. The result is a shift in both their perspectives, and the relationship grows stronger.

Often, just a few words can turn an entire situation around. Two communications consultants, a woman and a man, meet with a union steward, an ex-longshoreman, for the first time. They introduce themselves and say they are interested in helping the plant. The steward's comment is, *So, you're here to take us like sheep to the slaughter.* He literally shakes with anger and continues, *We had other consultants before, and they were a married couple too.* One of them seizes the opportunity and responds, *We're married but not to each other.* The rejoinder shatters his assumptions about them, and he agrees to sit down and hear what they have to say. A casual comment has thrown him into a new reality. From this inauspicious beginning, they form a productive and genuine relationship. The consultants' new friend proves quite agreeable to new ways of thinking about the plant, his relationship to the supervisors, and the personnel department. He even undertakes a sophisticated and productive project to include workers' feedback in supervisor's evaluations.

The rearrangement of even a few assumptions allows significant shifts throughout an entire way of thinking, thereby opening new possibilities.

Twenty-first-century thinking holds that communication consists of attempts to bridge the gap between one person's system or interpretive framework and another person's.

The ability to hear how others are listening allows you to address their concerns powerfully.

Suppose you are to meet the head of the union at a manufacturing plant. The word is that he is a troublemaker. Everyone warns you to watch your back or he will betray you. Against that background can the person do or say anything that will not be construed as making trouble? If he makes a conciliatory gesture, you may suspect it is a sinister set-up for trouble-making later. This man's reputation has tainted your listening. Whatever he does will confirm your suspicions and hold them in place at the same time. As Edward de Bono[1] writes:

It is historical continuity that maintains most assumptions— not a repeated assessment of their validity.

But what if you simply refuse to believe the scuttlebutt? You can alter someone's reputation by refusing to parrot the common wisdom and by instead speaking about them from another viewpoint. Questions and gentle yet persistent suggestions work best. *Are you sure Mike is really like that? He wasn't that way to me this morning.* If you phrase alternate interpretations, not confrontationally or stridently, but with open and honest questions, people have the opportunity to reassess and reach a new estimation of the union leader on their own. They may not even attribute the changes to their altered listening. *You know it's amazing how Mike has changed. Instead of being disruptive, he is being really helpful.* Mike, of course, has not changed at all. Instead, the context, the way in which people listen to Mike, has shifted.

Is there a way to use questions to shift how people listen? Might questions work better than statements of position?

---

[1]Edward de Bono, *Lateral Thinking*, Harper and Row, 1970.

TWELVE STEPS FOR DISSOLVING DISPUTES

The secret of transforming destructive disputes into productive collaboration is to alter the background interpretations and assumptions of the parties in such a way that the issue under dispute becomes irrelevant. The result is that arguments disappear, discord withers, and generosity emerges between people.

This section gives a 12-point approach to making this transformation happen. These steps are a specific application of the framework in our previous book, THE PHOENIX AGENDA: POWER TO TRANSFORM YOUR WORKPLACE. It is not necessary to be familiar with that framework to use this section, but if you are familiar with THE PHOENIX AGENDA, you will recognize its steps, although with different order and emphases.

Here is an example of what is possible using this 12-point agenda. A large midwestern public school system is facing a strike. The word is out to teachers, *If you are thinking about buying a car soon, wait. A strike is coming.* The school board and the administration are beside themselves. This is the death knell for the schools and the city. The last holdouts of the middle class will flee to the suburbs and those left behind will be poor, disabled, or elderly. The board members are sick at the thought and angry with the teachers' union. *They cannot possibly care about the children. We must put children first.* A concerned chamber of commerce, desperate to halt the erosion of the inner city, commissions an independent report on the state of the schools. The report concludes that extensive management rights have been given away to the teachers. The chamber insists the board must reclaim their authority. The local newspaper gets wind of the study and pressures the chamber to publish the report before city-wide balloting to renew the school levy. The paper prints an accusation from the teachers that the firm hired for the study is known for attempted union busting. Additional articles document the teachers' demands for an immediate 14 percent raise and the teachers' fears for their safety in the classroom. Everyone speaks with bitter recriminations against the other parties. Yet just a few months later the negotiations are amicably settled with a two-year extension of the current contract. The strike is averted, and the community turns its attention to building a school system that is a model for excellence. The issues of management rights, contract stripping, and union busting seem far away, and everyone is generous in their praise and acknowledgment of the other parties.

What happened? Did these protagonists actually find common ground to work together? The answer is yes, they did, and they did so quickly.

Disputes are dissolved by creating a context in which personal perspectives can grow, transform, and synergize.

The focus of each step is never on the issue itself, rather it is on the background of understanding, the mindset, the mental structures, the personal perspectives that make the issue be an issue at all. Therefore, some of the steps may seem indirect at first. This indirectness is a unique feature of the 21st-century approach. Twentieth-century thinkers take direct action on issues. Twenty-first-century thinkers focus on the context surrounding the issues.

Shift the Context, Not the Content

Have you noticed that the longer a quarrel continues, the less likely there will be a reconciliation? Even when specific issues are taken care of, new grievances seemingly spring from nowhere when the perspectives of the antagonists have not shifted. To solve significant disputes, we cannot continue to think about them in the same way we already think about them. The old way is not sufficient. If it were, the dispute would be already settled. For example, the union stewards at one foundry are convinced one of the managers is a hatchet man, brought in to automate and cruelly downsize the department. To focus on the stated problem by protesting the man's innocence is unlikely to change anyone's opinion of him. Clever staging of events to show the manager in a happy light will not help, either. The underlying issue is the stewards' sense of helplessness over their future. What will happen to them? Where will they find jobs? Restore their power and faith in themselves, and they will give the manager a chance to prove himself.

The labor relations director for an international corporation has spent 40 years in the business of negotiating union contracts. In his words, *Whatever the issue is about, it is never money, even when everyone says it is money. I hear about strikes over wage demands and I know it is not so.*

In any dispute, the presenting issue is never the true source of the conflict.

Failure to recognize this fact can result in actions that only make things worse. For example, a manufacturing plant, anxious to improve workforce relationships and productivity, brings in experts who attack the productivity and negotiating problems directly by taking over. The experts run all the meetings. They act as sole go-betweens in negotiations. They push specific agendas and solutions using their position and power to gain agreement. As a consequence, relations at the plant actually get worse. Underlying issues are not being addressed and the entire plant expresses a pent-up anger that jeopardizes its own future.

Focusing directly on the problem will not uncover a solution.

The question becomes, then, where to concentrate attention to foster the disappearance of the dispute. In the matter of wage disputes, the labor relations director points out that the issue is nearly always lack of respect or some other quality of human relationship. The place to focus is not on wages at all, but on building mutual respect among members of the workplace community.

In the school system, everyone is upset about so-called *management rights*. According to the school administration, the union has stolen away the power of management. In each school building, for example, there is not just a principal but also a union head. Major decisions and initiatives require the agreement and support of both. The school administration is convinced they must wrest back the authority that is rightfully theirs. The union, meanwhile, is convinced that this initiative is designed to strip the contract and reduce the teachers once again to the role of second-class participants in the school system. This interpretation is made worse by a report, funded by the chamber of commerce, that concludes the existing contracts take away many of the powers and privileges of management.

Unbeknownst to the protagonists, their whole debate revolves around an outmoded, 20th-century concept of management rights. As the 21st century approaches, the metaphor for management itself is changing. Management by dictum and fiat is being replaced by empowerment and driving decision making to the lowest possible level. The administration is basing its approach on a style and philosophy of management that is passé! Clearly the point of leverage in this situation is to inquire into, not which specific management rights ought to be wrested and resisted, but rather what management rights are to begin with, what are their value and limitations, and why one would want them in the first place. After all, there are alternate management styles that rely on enrollment, context, coaching, and listening. The moment of truth for one school board member comes in a flash, *Why, if we practiced modern management, our entire negotiating position for the contract would shift. We wouldn't be demanding management rights back, we'd be giving them away as fast as possible!* This board member's insight and her subsequent willingness to share it have a profound effect on the negotiations.

This example shows what is possible when dispute resolution focuses, not on the issues themselves, but on the nexus of assumptions and filters, on the differences in personal perspectives, that hold the dispute in place. When participants' personal perspectives shift, they can begin productive communication.

If you enable a shift to occur in the way the protagonists view the world, they will work out the dispute themselves and generate the skills to dissolve future disputes.

Live in the Future, Not in the Past

Twentieth-century thinking places the source of the future in mechanistic causes largely outside of individual human control. We are at the mercy of forces, causes, and trends outside of ourselves. *America is no longer the land of opportunity. Twenty-five percent of the boomer generation will have a difficult and erratic economic path through life.* These and similar statements from 20th-century experts who show their disbelief in the power of people to create their own destiny and to alter their prognosticated future by bold action.

Twenty-first-century thinking holds that, since humans create the world, they can also change it. Instead of mouthing dismal prognostications, people with faith in the future get on with building it. Faith in the future can never be proven or disproven since by the time the future comes to pass, it is no longer the future. Faith in the future, therefore, is outside the realm of objective discourse. Innovative solutions always and only spring from simple faith that some new result, some new world, some new course of action is available if only we are open to it.

> The essence of 21st-century mediation is to make available a sense that things could and can be different.

The day after learning about the power of their speaking and listening, about personal perspectives, and about possibility, the union heads and the management at one plant hold their regular meeting. Historically, such meetings are miserable, contentious affairs with nasty comments and bulging veins revealing rising blood pressure. Today's meeting is different. The fearsome business agent, a legendary man and veteran of strikes, uncharacteristically opens the meeting with a compliment to the personnel manager. The meeting takes on the grace of slow motion. People speak of possibility—*maybe we could bring the work of a distribution center to the plant, maybe we could have our people run the cafeteria and plow the snow, instead of laying them off. Maybe, even, we could leverage our new-found respect for one another to change the perception of this entire town as tough union—anti investment. Good heavens, if people believed that, maybe the dying downtown could be revitalized. We could actually have a role, could affect the entire community.* People are astonished that they can create such productive and inspiring plans together. They linger, anxious to continue these pleasant and promising interactions. The room seems lighter and warmer although it is midwinter. These people are experiencing what we call *living in the future.* It takes discipline and effort to make these visions come to pass. But without the visions, no altered future is possible.

Capitalize on Crisis

In late 1995, the school board faces a crisis. Contract negotiations are impending, relationships with the unions are terrible, and a strike looms. The board fears no one can help heal the relationships at this eleventh hour. Fortunately, instead of giving up, the members seek outside help.

If only we did not have to wait for a crisis before trying something new. But maybe crises are the only events powerful enough to cause us to question our beliefs and alter our approaches. As corporate manager Peter Conklin said shortly before his death:

> Thank heavens for the last minute. Without it nothing would ever get done.

Having faced the crisis head-on and asked for outside help, the board members find themselves miraculously empowered. All agree, *It is critical to delay negotiations, extend the existing contract, and work on improving the relationship.* The superintendent, showing initiative and leadership, meets personally with the union heads to extend a feeler. Two of the three bargaining units are interested. Further conversations initially look promising, then the talks stall. Each time, the superintendent courageously finds another way to open another conversation. He refuses to listen to members of his staff who tell him further efforts are futile. Finally the attorneys indicate that the union wants a two-year

extension rather than one year. This seeming breakthrough (being offered more than you asked for) creates another crisis because it is so far
outside of expectations. *No,* the attorneys insist, *we cannot possibly do
that. They must have something up their sleeves!* But the superintendent decides to trust, to take the offer at face value. Then, finally, the sought-
after extension appears within grasp, but the teachers want an additional
half-percent raise. The superintendent asserts, *There is no more money to
give. By law we cannot exceed our budget. If I do so, it could put me in jail.* Of
course, projecting tax revenues is always a matter of playing with pa-
rameters and formulas. The superintendent's new consultants ask only
one question, *Are the teachers worth the raise? Of course!* the superintendent responds. In the end he personally meets with the union representatives and over the protests of his negotiating team, agrees to the union's
request. The contract is extended for two years. Forty-thousand children
will not be out on the streets. The city has a chance to rebuild its image,
its reality. The head of the school board says, *The settlement is a miracle.*
The superintendent is a man with the weight of the world lifted off his
shoulders. Twentieth-century thinkers may claim he sold out. But he
knows he has fulfilled his obligation to the children of the city.

*They're doing it to us again. Here we are at a class to talk about chang-
ing our relationship with management and I get a call they want to announce
all these job changes. It just doesn't stop.* With that, the union chairman asks
if he can take time from the meeting to discuss the latest management
maneuver with his committee. Only this time is different. This time the
consultants offer to coach him and the committee. The result is that a
skeptical union committee chooses to meet with the plant manager the
next day to discuss the announcement. *It isn't the change so much as the
timing,* they explain to him. *Actually, what you have designed probably is the
best way. But it sure would be better to allow some employees to look it over
and come to their own conclusion. Otherwise they feel like they've been had.* To
their amazement, the plant manager agrees to their request. Then, in the
weeks that follow, grievances throughout the plant plummet.

Every crisis contains the seeds of a breakthrough.

Listen for Nobility in Everyone

If you shake hands, count your fingers! someone cautions when the consultants are invited to dinner with the teachers' union president. Again and again the consultants are warned this man is not to be trusted. They prepare for their dinner with a simple agreement to have a good time. This proves easy as the president and his wife are engaging conversationalists. During the evening the president brings up the issues in the school district and talks about his vision for the professionalization of the teachers. He admits his puzzlement over the furor his vision seems to create for the principals and the central administrators. The consultants have not sought or set up this moment but it demands their frank response. They counsel the president to be reconciled with the superintendent and the head of the principals' union. He makes no agreement to do so but expresses his appreciation for their forthrightness. The evening is a success and would have been even if business had not been discussed. The teachers' union president is a visionary, a dedicated teacher and professional, a man with much to contribute to peacemaking in the school district.

Theologians and philosophers have debated endlessly about the essential nature of human beings. Are we basically good, evil, or somewhere in between? Recall the discussion in Chapter 6 about how language creates reality. *The workers in this plant are all jerks. They are lazy and don't deserve the pay they get. I want to replace all of them with machines*, says an engineer. Is this a statement of fact or does it create a reality? How hard would you work for someone who spoke about you in this way?

Listen for the nobility of people. Speak about that.

People say a lot of things about me and about what I have said about you. Most of it is not true. But whether true or not, it is past. I appreciate what you have done. You are trying to do to improve this plant. You have made good choices in the managers you have hired. You have my support. With those words to the plant manager, the union committee chairman uses the power of his position to turn around the union-management relationship at the plant. What he says is true because he says so.

The workers at the mill across town are profoundly discouraged. Their ranks thinned due to years of relentless automation, they see only more of the same for the future. They express their helplessness in the only way that seems available—sullen and reluctant compliance. They express their anger by trashing their break room, leaving it constantly littered with wrappers and chocolate milk cartons, infuriating their plant manager.

And yet these same workers are part of proud traditions and serve a vital role. They mill flour, which makes bread, which is the staff of life. Their mill is the largest soft-wheat flour mill in the world. On their efforts depend the fortunes of one of the best-known brand names on the planet. Their attention to quality and detail graces the meals of virtually everyone in the United States as well as in many other countries. These workers are union men and women. Though they have forgotten their own heritage, the tradition of which they are a part is one of courage and contribution. The end of child labor, the enactment of workplace safety standards, and even simple respect for the dignity of labor: these things society owes to unions.

No one has told the workers these things, not for a long time. In a burst of insight, one manager takes his workers on a trip—a simple visit to the bakery 200 miles away where the flour is turned into biscuits, cookies, and bread. The workers who take the trip are amazed. *This is where our flour goes and what it does?* They are filled with pride and establish informal, cooperative relationships with their bakery counterparts to pack the trucks and to load the cars in such a way that they can be more easily unloaded. They redouble their efforts to mill a more consistent flour, for inconsistently milled flour may rise too much, making biscuits that will not fit properly into the packaging.

This exceptional manager has the wisdom to realize that his people need to be reminded of the dignity and value of their work, in a way that they can appreciate and hear. There is no more important realization for leaders in the 21st-century workplace.

Create Wisdom, Not Answers

Ultimately, all that we learn is about ourselves. Whatever the field of study, it leads us back to our personal development. Creating a context for learning allows people the opportunity to reshape and expand their personal perspectives. As a result of her success with a personally intimidating project, the woman in the following example finds heretofore-hidden skills to apply to school district issues.

A member of the school board wants to learn the use of electronic mail on her home computer. She enlists a coach for this project who asks her to send him an e-mail to demonstrate her success. To someone who has long used e-mail or is at ease with technology, this project sounds simple enough. For this woman, with reservations about computer technology, sending e-mail is a major achievement. She is so pleased with the outcome that she uses her first e-mail to request coaching on a meeting she has arranged. This meeting, it turns out, is to bring together teachers and administrators to work out a process to assure teachers access to classrooms when school is not in session. This access has been the source of flare-ups during the year. Her meeting is a success and noted by the participants as a remarkable and productive session. Later, during the contract-extension talks, she sees the desirability of addressing some of the teachers' concerns, such as safety, outside of the contract. Perhaps a similar meeting will work. She contacts the teachers and administrators and receives a positive response. All parties ask her to take charge, and she agrees, removing this sensitive issue as a roadblock and opening it up for immediate attention.

In the same district, the head of the school board is desperately concerned to avoid a strike in the district. At first her coach does not talk with her about strategies for avoiding strikes at all. Instead he asks about her personal interests. It turns out that she is active in a community theater that once prospered but is now suffering from a lack of volunteers. She asks for help with a project to recruit volunteers. Her first step is to call some of the volunteers who have dropped out to discover their reasons. This is something she has never done. Through these simple phone calls, she learns that some people dropped out because no one greeted them when they showed up to work on the last performance. Others dropped out because no one complimented them on their art work for the sets. Through these conversations, she learns a great deal and lures many disaffected volunteers back. Not only that, but by sharing her project with her peers, another school board member puts her in touch with a organization of 5000 retired citizens ready and willing to be involved in the artistic life of the community, if only someone will show them a way. In the school board president's own words, *I realized how important it is to actually ask what is going on and listen to the answer I get. It is so much simpler to fix the right problem.* Her compelling personal experience in revitalizing the community theater affects her behavior and contributes to dissolving the threatened school strike. Two months later when a nasty rumor circulates about the teachers' union, this woman calls the teachers' chief negotiator to find out what is actually happening and to help quash the rumor as quickly as she can. Without this call, the negotiations to extend the contract could have collapsed.

> Teach people new skills in an area that has compelling interest and immediate personal benefit to them. They will, of their own accord, generalize these skills to the workplace.

Take the Risk to Trust

For the dispute to end, the protagonists must choose to trust one another. The 20th-century view of trust is as a record of accounts. *If I come through for you I earn a trust point. If I fail I lose two trust points. Whether or not you trust me depends upon my balance in the trust account that you maintain on me.* Of course, no one comes through 100 percent of the time and so none of us deserves to be completely trusted. There is also the problem that it is mentally difficult to keep an accurate trust balance for every one of the thousands of people we interact with in our lifetimes.

The 21st-century alternative is to consider trust not as a result, but as a source. Of all the desirable qualities in a healthy society or a productive and nurturing workplace, trust is the most critical. Can any of us do our best work in a situation where there is no trust? What is possible in a group where there is complete trust?

What if trust always originates from someone taking the risk to give it as a gift?

You can generate trust by how you listen and speak, taking a risk, putting yourself on the line. For example, you can ask people to give you a chance to prove yourself. A consultant facing this situation is acutely aware of the need to establish rapport and trust between the union representatives and herself. She asks what will enable them to work with her. She offers to resign from the project at any time they wish for her to do so. She even offers to provide the union committee chairman with a signed resignation letter for his keeping, if that will make a difference. In the end, they ask her only to keep private their conversations, and she assures them she will do that. They leave the conversation open, with the understanding that anyone of them can raise the matter of trust with her at any time. At the end of the meeting she knows that she has been given the gift of their trust.

At the core of trust may be simply the willingness to keep the conversation alive.

Concerned about the effect of negativism and the superficiality of rhetoric on our democracy, a political science professor from the University of Texas at Austin tries a remarkable experiment. His core concept is the idea of discourse, reasoned and informed discussion in which people show respect for others' views, listen to and learn from one another, and create together, better opinions, solutions, and programs of action than they could have by themselves.

So with the help of public television and an assortment of sup-
porters, he flies 600 randomly selected U.S. citizens, all expenses paid,
to Austin to participate in the National Political Issues Forum. There
they meet in small discussion groups exchanging views and gaining insight into the others' perspectives and concerns. Following that, the
delegates meet with a panel of nationally prominent experts on issues of
the economy, family and values, and foreign policy. Later they meet in
open forum with several candidates for president. At the end of this
time together, a delegate to the convention, a chicken farmer, says after
meeting with his fellow citizens, *Well, I expected a lot of disagreements,
but I was surprised to discover we all want pretty much the same thing.*

Public negative sound bites swirl around the school district in late
1995. *Teachers fire the first salvo* and *Chamber poisons bargaining climate*
scream through the headlines and permeate in-group conversations. Reasoned discourse among the parties does not exist. The head of one union
admits that he has not met privately with the superintendent for over a
year. When contract extension talks begin, the tone shifts. Once the parties actually sit down in a situation conducive to reasoned discourse, they
discover, in their own words, *Everyone actually wants the same thing.*

Open-minded discourse with other people generates trust.

Co-Design Strategies

AT&T is executing, in 1996, a force management program, their term for
40,000 layoffs. Their strategy is meticulous and well planned. Workers
must first prepare a two-page resume, detailing all their work experience
and skills. Then the manager, now called a coach, rates the skills on a
scale of one to four. Based on these ratings, the company offers the employee a voluntary severance package. If the employee refuses the offer,
a committee of managers, including an outside consultant, reviews the
resume, making decisions about who stays and who goes. If you go, you
are given a termination date, a severance check, and allowed to use a

company-funded outplacement facility that includes telephones, job postings, a cubicle, and office equipment.

As strategies go, AT&T is trying. Anxious to preserve some of its tradition as a family-oriented company, and to retain the loyalty of those remaining, it goes to costly lengths to help the departees. The Personnel department phrases the entire process in new language: *force management, coaching, roundtable reviews, redressing the imbalance of forces or skills, unassigned.*[2] The head of Personnel explains that the world's workforce is now contingent, that permanent jobs no longer exist anywhere, and that people must be their own entrepreneurs. Yet critics charge that the company is simply treating workers like disposable tools. The employees, whose loyalty the company is trying to maintain, are very upset.

Maybe the problem is that the layoff strategy was not participatively designed. The strategy is conceived entirely by top managers, without input from those who are affected. Billed as a move to reduce bureaucracy, the company sets up a 3,000 personnel bureaucracy, exempt from the layoffs, to administer the program. By contrast, 21st-century strategies are inclusive: They give everyone a chance to contribute ideas, and to share risk and rewards. Rhino Foods, in Vermont, makes cookie dough for Ben and Jerry's ice cream. In 1992, Ben and Jerry's sales decline, strongly affecting Rhino's cash flow. An ordinary company would lay people off. Rhino's managers instead call a meeting of the entire company. They explain the situation and admit they do not know what to do. They invite the entire company to brainstorm strategies for solving the problem. Hundreds of people break into groups and give free reign to their creativity. Thousands of ideas are generated—the raw material of possibility. One of the thousands of ideas rises to the surface. Instead of laying people off, contract them out to competitors and hire them back when business improves. The company does this. More than enough workers volunteer for the career-enriching experience of spending six months working for another company. The six months over, the market for ice cream recovers and there is a job for everyone who wants to come back. Those who do come back bring new expertise to Rhino, increasing its competitive position. Everyone wins, no one is hurt. Such is the power of inclusive strategizing.

2"Don't Go Away Mad, Just Go Away," by Edmund L. Andrews, *The New York Times*, Feb. 13, 1996, D1ff.

Some companies talk about their workers as *them* and some talk about their workers as *us*. A company based on the idea of *us* has an enormous advantage. Such a company has access to the full knowledge, talents, and insights of its people and can hammer out strategy through productive dialog. Instead of one party dictating to the other what must be done, all parties can pool their intellectual resources to create better plans than either could come up with by themselves.

Consider this scenario. Managers and union leaders are working closely together designing the future for the plant. An aspect of their vision is that the number of jobs in the plant will increase. Brainstorming produces the idea to move from a three-shift to a four-shift operation, which requires additional employees, thus creating new jobs. The managers support the idea enthusiastically. However, a fourth shift also decreases the overtime required from employees. There is a tense moment when the union chairman reacts, *Our members will never go for that. They count on overtime pay. It will never work. We'll be creamed if we propose that idea! Just forget it.* With that, the suggestion is immediately eliminated from the list. Everyone assumes that adding a shift means people must make less money although the company will save money. Everyone also assumes that it is up to the union committee to sell the idea to the employees. But the two sides keep talking. During the next break, one manager asks the union leader, *What if we could assure people they would make the same money? Perhaps a raise, or a guarantee to match last year's income? Something to ensure the senior people do not take a pay hit.* The union chairman tilts his head and chuckles, *Well, now that is a whole new ball game. We could certainly talk about that!*

Create a Framework for Action

Remember the worker who went home for the whole day because he was docked one attendance point for being 15 minutes late to work? The leverage to improve worker and management morale in this situation is not to apply more pressure but to inquire into and alter the context. The tension in this example is obvious. Management feels workers need coercion to perform, so they negotiate punitive attendance systems. The workers feel like underlings, manipulated by a system out of their control. So they just get mad or give up.

For one plant, a breakthrough in worker-management relations comes when the personnel manager leaves for another job. This gives management the opportunity to include the workers in the interviewing and selection process for the new personnel manager. The workers are astonished, never having been involved in a hiring decision before. They participate and make their selection, which management honors. Now, though the personnel rules are the same, grievances decrease dramatically and attendance improves. What has happened is that the context, the level of trust has improved, so that requests for action can be heard.

> Participation generates ownership. Ownership generates dignity. Dignity generates responsibility.

An effective, nontraditional method for improving the workplace is to get people involved, not in activities directly relevant to the workplace at all, but rather in compelling personal projects where they can practice action skills and realize personal benefits. These skills then automatically transfer to the workplace. For example, one worker, as a hobby, builds motorized go-carts for his son. The two of them race these carts at local meets on the weekends. The worker's problem is to find money to finance this hobby. So a friend offers to coach him, and he accepts. They hit upon a plan to sell sponsorships to local businesses. The business gets its logo or decal on the cart and on the truck that transports it, in exchange for a fee. The worker approaches local stores and restaurants to ask them for sponsorships. Within two weeks, he astounds himself by raising $2,500. And critically, he has honed a new skill to use at work—how to ask people to do things in a way that makes the positive benefits clear to them.

One company is concerned that the employees do not take initiative. Instead of issuing a directive about initiative, the vice president prints up a limited number of permission slips. Each slip reads: *The bearer of this slip has permission to take a risk, to exceed their authority, and to contribute unexpected results to the company—signed (vice president).* The permission slips quickly become a hot commodity, and people start new initiatives, one of which generates an unplanned million-dollar profit in six weeks.

With a framework for action in place, people will act boldly. Sometimes management fears that if workers are too much empowered, they will question management authority or even be empowered to find jobs elsewhere. They may, but if management fulfills its fundamental mission, then the workplace is one where people feel valued and want to remain.

Break the Addiction to Work

I went home at 5 last night and boy, was that ever an eye opener. My daughter's friend wanted to know what I was doing home! Then my wife asked if I had been fired. I think I need to get home for dinner more often. Those are the words of a plant manager who is on the verge of confronting his addiction to work. It looks to him as though it really is the work that keeps him in the office night after night. When he begins a project to make it home at least two nights a week for dinner, he is amazed that he can do so.

Addictive systems are created by each of us and then we cling to the rightness of the system we have developed. The miracle of being human is our ability to create reality, to literally create our world. The tragedy of being human may be that, once our world is created, we become habituated to it. For the manager and millions of workers today, there is a belief in some external force or pressure that drives them to work long and tiring hours week after week. Superficially the cost appears personal for him and his family. Yet when this manager learns to go home at night, it has an amazing impact on the people who work for him. Where once the supervisors dumped their issues on him at the end of the day, now they speak to him earlier to help him leave on time. They have a greater sense of their power to make decisions without him and feel better about leaving on time themselves. The ripple effect through the department infuses each person with a sense of gratitude, privilege, and responsibility toward their own jobs.

Shift the Medium that Describes the Problem

Language itself holds our personal perspectives in place. Often in disputes, the problem is simply the lack of an appropriate communication medium. Simply shifting the language used to describe a situation can break up strongly held opinions and preconceptions, as the following case demonstrates.

At a cereal plant, there are many grievances, and the vast majority of these are related to overtime rules. The plant, which looks to the uninitiated like a neo-Gothic set from a *Batman* movie, runs 24 hours a day in three shifts. Forklifts zip around stacks of cartons the size of small city blocks. Cookers rise 14 feet in the air, and enormous guns shoot and puff the cereal. To keep everything running profitably, the corporate office monitors supply and demand and delicately balances work among its 14 plants nationwide. The raw material for the plants is agricultural produce, which by its nature varies in availability, quality, and price. Consumer tastes are capricious, and demand for products changes rapidly. Consequently, the corporate office often orders shifts in production at the last minute.

To keep the plant running 24 hours per day, in the face of ever-changing supply and demand, is an art. Never shutting down unplanned and always running at peak require constant change in the number and skills of the people who run the machinery. Over the years this union plant has established a complex set of rules about who is to be given the opportunity for extra work. This cuts both ways. If an individual wants extra work and is first in line, he or she is required by contract to be the first called. On the other hand, if someone offered the opportunity for extra work declines, under the right circumstances, he or she can be *forced* to work.

The set of rules about who must be called and in what order is immensely complex. The rules exist as a body of customs, expectations, and practices—in both written and oral tradition. The personnel department, the supervisors, and the managers make, in the opinion of the workers, constant errors, which are then written up as formal complaints or grievances. These grievances are expensive. A joint union-management committee of 12 people struggles to resolve them internally. If the committee decides in favor of the employee, the company must pay the person as though they had worked. This is called *pay for time not worked.* If no agreement is reached through the internal procedure, both sides hire lawyers and take the matter to outside arbitration.

It turns out that the rules for overtime are simply represented in the wrong medium. They are spelled out in linear contract language that fails to do justice to the idiosyncrasies and complexity of individual cases. For example, the personnel office telephones a worker who is, correctly, first on the list. His wife answers and says he is not interested. So the office calls the next person on the list. Later, the worker grieves because, according to him, the office should not have taken his wife's say-so. Nothing in the contract covers this situation.

Someone proposes to the union and management leaders to represent the overtime rules, not as contractual language, but rather as a series of flow diagrams. A committee convenes and maps out the overtime rules in pictures. Once the rules are captured and presented in an appropriate medium, much of the ambiguity dissolves. The result is an overnight reduction in the number of grievances relating to scheduling. Able to see the rules laid out, union and management begin to discuss how to dramatically simplify them.

Another example, from an entirely different industry, also shows the power of changing the medium or language in which a particular reality is represented. End-user software is more easily learned and used when it is designed with consistent conventions. Conversely, creative engineers are often anxious to place their individual stamp on the end product. This practice can make it difficult for a large company to design software programs that have the same look and feel for the user.

One software company facing this problem tries to solve it by the 20th-century approach of laying down rules and procedures. Independent-minded engineers rebel at this approach, which backfires. The problem is solved using an approach outside the authoritarian conceptual frame. The software company arranges a computer-interface exhibit. Hundreds of engineers working on the project fly in to participate in the event, a flamboyant *show and tell* where everyone displays and views the different programs and styles. These informal interactions and cross-cultural exchanges successfully create a common usage of software style across the entire company.

> Unusual ways of representing and displaying the content of the work can resolve disputes and open the way to creative possibilities and actions.

Conclude and Close the Past

As disputes are always about the past, never about the present, finding a way to put the past to rest has great leverage in finding resolution. All disputes are tiresome reruns and replays of past grievances. Remember that obnoxious couple you go to dinner with that reminds you of Liz Taylor and Richard Burton in *Who's Afraid of Virginia Woolf?* They spend the whole evening reminding and embarrassing one another, for the benefit of you as audience, about past misdeeds and deficiencies. The British and Irish bomb and persecute each other in endless replays of disputes originated by people dead for hundreds of years.

Completing the past means putting it to rest, putting it behind you, and getting on with productive, positive living. That we are not better at doing this is a profound misfortune for all of us. We hang on to past grievances and slights, as Jack Nicholson says in the quote that begins this chapter. But completion, like all other aspects of human reality, is created through language. It is over when you say it is over. And only you can say.

Follow the example of this remarkable union leader who says to his union stewards: *A lot went on in the past. But it's a new group of managers here now and what happened before isn't their fault. You can't blame them. We want a new future for us, too. So you've got to forget about what happened before.* His words do not fall on deaf or passive ears. The stewards burst out with arguments and reasons why the new approach simply will not work. *The first thing a new supervisor does is to read the personnel files. That isn't letting go of the past. What are you going to do about that?* For more than an hour the objections fly across the room. The chairman goes on to tell the stewards to work with the supervisors and settle grievances whenever they can. In the end, they leave the room and do exactly as he asks. They let go of the past and begin building a future. Within a few months, the constant references to management's past offenses disappear from plant gossip.

The superintendent of the school district has suffered many blows and insults during his term in office. Most of them, he feels, come with the title. A few, the personal ones, have hurt him deeply and are hard for him to forget or forgive. Yet he does. He sets aside the pain for the sake of the children and the educational system. He praises his detractors for their capabilities and strengths. He acknowledges their leadership in the schools and appreciates their support. This courageous choice enables him to show the generosity to reach an agreement with the unions. He achieves completion and retires with honor.

Gratitude Is the Key to Results

Ancient wisdom teaches that gratitude is the highest of all virtues. Yet 20th-century thinkers are never satisfied, let alone grateful, with or for last quarter's results. Instead the results are used to shame the short-comers and to set higher hurdles for the high performers.

The tragedy of the 20th century is a loss of gratitude. We do not recognize our results. Even the greatest achievements are lost if they are not crystallized in our thinking and speaking. The context for realizing results may be nothing more than the opportunity for people themselves to say what has been achieved, and in so doing, create an oral history of events.

What follows is the new history spoken by employees from the organizations whose experiences figure throughout this book.

Things have changed, one committeeman says. *Everyone wants to help.*

Another committee member is now a trainer for the automated work systems introduced into the plant. She is committed to see that everyone is able to learn the new equipment and processes.

An African-American committeeman starts his career at the plant years ago. He faces ghastly racial discrimination—shunned in the lunch room, tires slashed in the parking lot. But today, as a respected engineer and union committee member, he expresses gratitude, not bitter resentment. *Who would have thought that I would be so well-respected today?*

If I held a grudge against everyone who had wronged me, I wouldn't have many people left to speak with, would I? Today, this man is in constant demand throughout the plant to dissolve diversity issues. *They say I have a calming effect and a way of getting to the bottom of things,* he says.

Two union committee members have made peace with one another, burying a years-old hatchet that kept them from synergizing their efforts.

And the much-feared business agent, veteran of many strikes, observes, in a reflective moment, *I can retire now. This plant means so much to me and I was afraid that if I leave it will close. For the first time I see you can go on without me and the plant will be just fine.*

At the school district, the superintendent talks about the kindness shown to him by the union heads and the future prospects for the district. *I am filled with gratitude that seems to grow each day. It reminds me of what life is all about.*

In the words of another manager, *I cannot express the gift this has been for my family. My cares are not so heavy now and my wife and I feel like newlyweds.*

DISPUTES AND WORLD PEACE

Disputes exist, always and only, because protagonists are operating in a restricted context. The way in which they speak and listen to each other creates a limited reality within which destructive competition is the only available option. As in a vicious cycle, the competition in turn rigidifies and limits the perceived reality. As with all human realities, this cycle is held in place by the language people use to describe it. The leverage is a change in language. The 12 points discussed above discourage language (listening and speaking) that holds limited realities in place and encourage language that creates new possibilities for exploration. If you can create a context—a new playground—big enough, then the antagonists will come together, almost on their own, and they will invent new relationships.

The ideas in this chapter have worked well in traditionally contentious and difficult environments—marriages and union-management relations. Could they be applied more broadly? How many readers remember the meeting in Iceland between Ronald Reagan and Mikhail

Gorbachev? They talk, man to man, and actually create, between themselves, the possibility of the end of the Cold War. Perhaps you recall the terrified look on their faces on television as they leave that meeting. They confront true possibility and are afraid. Their advisors rush up to tell them they are premature, that such a possibility is unthinkable. Yet here we are at the end of the 20th century, and the Cold War is no more, thanks to the courage of, and discourse between, these two statesmen.

> More important than the decommissioning of weapons is the decommissioning of outdated perspectives.

Conclusion

Even a thought, even a possibility, can shatter us and transform us.

FRIEDRICH NIETZSCHE, *Eternal Recurrence*

We are at a crossroads in time. The current workplace upheaval has been characterized by many as the latest example of the organization exploiting the worker. Downsizing, rightsizing, and reengineering have been, according to some experts, *brutally applied, creating a climate of fear—another attempt by people at the top of the organization to maintain their own position and power.* Conversely, for executives and managers there are no easy answers about how the company is to keep up with unrelenting global competition or even survive. Companies and workers alike, we are in the midst of tumult that is not of our own choosing. Are we at the effect of forces we do not understand and cannot control? The 20th-century perspective says we are out-of-our-league, in over our heads and the situation will only get worse from here.

As workers, from the executive office to the factory floor, we have all seen difficult circumstances, many of which bear no relation to the macro-level marketplace changes in progress. In our careers we have suffered hurts, slights, and insults. We have been unappreciated, forgotten, and passed over. We have faced unfair and dishonest competitors who have tried to ruin us. Some of us have confronted direct and personal discrimination. We all have grievances, and they are all valid. No one can blame you, personally or professionally, for seeing yourself as a victim overcome by events you have not chosen.

But, what profit is there in this view? It may be that you have worked with unprincipled and incompetent people. It may be that someone does owe you a deep and sincere apology. It may be that you are tired of trying. One thing these perspectives will not allow you, however, is the freedom and joy that come with creating your own destiny.

In this country, we believe in freedom. We take pride that in our society, all people are free; no one's self-esteem need depend on economic background and upbringing. *You* earn *your* respect from what *you* do and who *you* are.

This struggle in which we find ourselves today appears to be economic in nature. But the struggle is more subtle than the need for jobs, better pay, and lifetime employment. The struggle is more fundamental than the question of whether particular companies, or particular ways of working, will survive. The struggle is not economic at all. We are engaged in a struggle for freedom from the mistaken belief that we are victims at the mercy of forces we cannot control. True freedom is the ability to trust in ourselves and our capabilities, to define who we are, and to create our own destiny. The essence of 21st-century thinking is that we are free to create what will happen next for ourselves.

But we do not live in a vacuum. Most of us work for businesses and institutions we do not own or autonomously run. And these too, are our creation. We express ourselves through our work; companies are a synthesis of the individual contributions and energies of all the employees. Even at work, the question remains the same:

Do circumstances happen to us or do we happen to circumstances?

Beyond business, we are members of a community in which each person holds a power to create equal to our own. Together, we create our communities, our economy, our country, and the entire world we share. What kind of world could we create if we, knowingly, set ourselves to the task?

FLIGHT OF THE PHOENIX has focused on the power of twenty-first-century thinking, expressed in listening and speaking. For your listening and speaking to create the world you want, you must choose to listen and speak responsibly. Responsible communication is listening for and speaking only what you want to create and then acting in a manner that is consistent with what you have said. This is known as *integrity*. There was a time when all matters of human interaction were supposed to be conducted on the basis of *integrity* or *word of honor*. It can be that way again.

I am my word. My word is my bond.

What would be possible if you absolutely always keep every promise you make? Or, admit and apologize for absolutely every promise you do not keep and then do not make insincere promises in the future? Your rebirth as a person of the 21st-century begins with your willingness to take upon yourself the responsibility to listen and speak in a manner consistent with what you wish to create.

The myth of the Phoenix is a fable of death and glorious rebirth that promises a greater fulfillment than before. THE FLIGHT OF THE PHOENIX is the story of fulfillment between the magical moments of birth and death. Born with wings, a bird flies. How will you express yourself? The 21st-century choice is to *listen* generously and to *speak* with integrity.

Sources

Some readers may be interested in the sources of our ideas, either to know where they originated or to have the ability to create their own applications of thinking based on philosophies that have stood the test of time. The ideas in this book come from our own experience but are viewed through a particular philosophical perspective sometimes called contextualism. We rely extensively on this philosophical outlook to add depth and consistency to our work.

The following is a brief bibliography, mostly of works on philosophy, that have been important to our perspective in writing this book.

Agar, Michael. *Language Shock: Understanding the Culture of Conversation.* New York: William Morrow, 1994.

Dewey, John. *The Philosophy of John Dewey.* Edited by J. J. McDermott. Chicago: University of Chicago Press, 1981.

Eisler, Riane. *The Chalice and the Blade: Our History, Our Future.* New York: HarperCollins, 1988.

Fox, Matthew. *The Reinvention of Work: A New Vision of Livelihood for Our Time.* New York: HarperCollins, 1994.

Goldsmith, Joel. *The Infinite Way.* Marina del Rey, CA: De Vorss & Company, 1947.

Heidegger, Martin. *Being and Time.* Translated by J. Macquarrie and E. Robinson. New York: Harper and Row, 1962.

_____. *On the Way to Language.* Translated by P. D. Hertz. New York: Harper and Row, 1971.

Palmer, Helen. *The Enneagram.* New York: HarperCollins, 1988.

Pepper, Stephen. *World Hypotheses.* Berkeley, CA: University of California Press, 1942.

Pirsig, Robert M. *Zen and the Art of Motorcycle Maintenance.* New York: William Morrow, 1974.

Watts, Alan. *The Way of Zen.* New York: Vintage Books, 1957.

Index

About the Authors

John Whiteside and Sandra Egli collaborate on writing and consulting. Both worked for large corporations before going into business for themselves.

John was originally trained as a psychologist and later switched to software engineering and management. Sandra's original background is in mathematics. She managed in a number of small companies before becoming a director at a major financial and travel services firm.

Since starting their own businesses, they have, together and separately, consulted with many Fortune 50 companies, with smaller businesses, and with organizations in the public sector. The focus of their work is always simultaneously boosting work results and quality of work life. They are especially interested in mediation and dispute dissolution.

Using modern technology, they find transcontinental collaborative work productive and enjoyable.

To learn more about the ideas in the book contact:

John Whiteside
Industrial Revolutions
234 North Road
Fremont, NH 03044
(603) 679-5443
75720.1406@compuserve.com
or at
johnw@tiac.net

Sandra Egli
Industrial Revolutions
1109 East Braeburn Drive
Phoenix, AZ 85022
(602) 942-1350
75047.2372@compuserve.com

Visit our home page at: http://www.industrialrevolution.com

CHESTER COLLEGE LIBRARY